WORLD WAR II CHRONICLES

THE AIR WAR

WORLD WAR II CHRONICLES

THE AIR WAR

BERNARD C. NALTY

Series Editor: Lieutenant Colonel Roger Cirillo, United States Army, Retired

MetroBooks

MetroBooks

An Imprint of Friedman/Fairfax Publishers

©1999 by Michael Friedman Publishing
Group, Inc.

Library of Congress Cataloging-in-Publication
Data available upon request.
ISBN 1-56799-758-9

Editor: Celeste Sollod
Art Director: Kevin Ullrich
Photography Editor: Amy Talluto
Production Manager: Camille Lee

Color separations by Ocean Graphic Arts Ltd.
Printed in China by Leefung Asco Printers Ltd.

10 9 8 7 6 5 4 3 2 1

For bulk purchases and special sales,
please contact:
Friedman/Fairfax Publishers
Attention: Sales Department
15 West 26th Street
New York, NY 10010
212/685-6610 FAX 212/685-1307

Visit our website:
http://www.metrobooks.com

Acknowledgments

Three persons have contributed
to the completion of this book:
my wife, Barbara; my editor,
Celeste Sollod; and the librarian
of the Air Force history program,
Yvonne Kincaid.

Contents

"A Factor in War"

Lt. Col. Roger Cirillo, United States Army, Retired

WHILE BEING INTERVIEWED IN 1906 ABOUT his flying machine, Wilbur Wright said, prophetically, "It will be a factor in war." This prediction would be proved true before too long. First used over Libya in 1912, the warplane became a fixture of war within two years, from World War I's very first battles on the western front to the end of that conflict.

During World War I, flying primitive aircraft at great risk, combat pilots added a new dimension to warfare. By war's end, aerial warfare had touched all its modern lineaments: strategic bombing, air superiority operations, aerial reconnaissance, battlefield attacks, and sea and land interdiction.

While no major power felt it could forgo possessing air power, each decided differently how that power could best be used. While air power visionaries saw the airplane as decisive in and of itself, conservative elements in the major armies and navies of the world saw the plane as an ancillary weapon to be used in supporting traditional forces. World War II tested both theories.

The air dimension became an essential element of waging war but by itself was generally not decisive. While Hitler's Luftwaffe was key in his early victories, the might and dash of his ground forces were necessary to conquer France and the Low Countries. Virtually every army found air superiority a necessary adjunct to large unit maneuvers, but not necessarily a guarantor of victory on the ground. Moreover, such countries as the United States and Great Britain, which possessed huge air fleets, found apportioning their forces a bitter experience. Some airmen who defined the airplane as a strategic and war-winning weapon of its own accord both resented and resisted supporting ground battles and flying offshore submarine patrols, claiming that any diversion from their "strategic mission" would lengthen the war.

The European Theater

Nowhere was this argument more bitter than in the European Theater, and perhaps, nowhere were the results more controversial. The round-the-clock bombing strategy of the Allies netted significant gains, and should be considered a major contributor to victory, virtually a campaign itself, like the war at sea or the war on land.

Germany found it necessary to devote nearly 900,000 personnel to defending the Reich's population and industries and fired countless millions of rounds of ammunition

Wilbur Wright's prediction that the airplane would become a factor in war came to fulfillment in bombers like this Boeing B-17G Flying Fortress, bristling with machine guns, that has just returned from a raid on German installations in Nazi-occupied France.

skyward from thousands of heavy guns, consuming ammunition, guns, and personnel that could have been used to great effect in ground combat. Moreover, with crippled transportation systems and oil supplies nearly dried up from bombing, even as German industry continued to produce war materials, delivery of much of these materials was delayed and, toward the end, made totally impossible.

Germany, however, was overrun on the ground, first because of the numbers and ferocity of the Red Army that fought the bulk of Germany's forces, and later thanks to Eisenhower's grinding offensive from the west. While no one can ever answer how inevitable the Allied victory in Europe would have been without the strategic bombing campaign, it is certain that the airmen were instrumental in helping to make the victory on the ground possible and in shortening the war.

Most controversial is the European air campaign's cost. Over 100,000 Allied airmen, mostly bomber crewmen, died as a result, as did unrecorded thousands of German fighter pilots. Estimated losses of German airmen on all fronts including those killed, wounded, missing, and taken prisoner, exceeded 100,000, all of whom fought unsuccessfully to stop waves of Allied bombers from reaching their targets. Air attacks on industries killed at least three quarters of a million civilians and devastated the major cities of Germany. The same types of devastation that German aircraft had wreaked on Guernica, Warsaw, London, and Coventry, the Allies later brought home to Berlin, Dresden, and Hamburg, with terrible vengeance.

The Pacific War

The Pacific war saw a different and perhaps more decisive use of air power. Beginning with an enemy air raid that sank most of the U.S. battleship fleet, the war ended with a single bomb—the most devastating weapon ever used.

Aircraft made fleets fatally vulnerable without a friendly air umbrella overhead, covered most of the nearly eighty amphibious landings made in the Pacific, and in the end, conducted a more devastating and brutal air offensive against Japan's cities than was seen over the course of the war in Europe.

While the early Pacific war seemed to cover distances too great for bomber fleets to hit the enemy's homeland, the massive firestorms sown by U.S. bombers in the war's final months made the invasion of Japan unnecessary as Japan's military production capability was totally destroyed. While never a replacement for the ship in the Pacific's great expanse, the airplane proved to be an equally valuable weapon in the Pacific in what was generally considered a naval war.

The Legacy of Air Power

The airplane left a stark legacy following World War II. Many of the war's most famous film images stem from the air war. Stuka dive-bombers symbolized the German blitzkrieg, and the well-known image of St. Paul's Cathedral in London surrounded by a swirl of flame portrayed to the world British resolve in enduring the German Blitz.

The startling portrait of a Chinese baby in Shanghai, a bombing victim, foretold the desolation that would come to many via aircraft, and the mushroom clouds photographed over Hiroshima and Nagasaki made real the ultimate devastation that was delivered by air. More than a million civilians died in bombings around the world, and their plight captured on newsreel screens and newspaper pages became common sights during, and after, the war.

Wilbur Wright's comment had proven all too true; the airplane did become a factor in war, but the horror that it brought exceeded even the air power enthusiasts' wildest predictions.

Aircraft carriers like the USS *Hornet*, namesake of a similar ship sunk by the Japanese in 1942, projected air power over the vastness of the Pacific, enabling U.S. Army and Marine Corps amphibious forces to seize airfields for land-based bombers within range of Japan. Grumman F6F fighters warm up for a strike against Tokyo in February 1945.

The Wings of Mars

CAPT. RICHARD VON BENTIVEGNI HAD unintentionally enabled the civilians of London to share some of the same dangers experienced by their sons on the western front of World War I. As he turned his five-engine biplane bomber toward its base in German-occupied Belgium on the night of January 28, 1918, he could see the glow of fires burning in London. He believed he had dropped a 660-pound (300kg) bomb squarely on the offices of Britain's Admiralty. The bomb had missed its intended target, however, passed through a grating next to a printing plant, and exploded in the basement, which was sheltering some five hundred people. The blast and resulting flame and smoke accounted for some of the thirty-eight killed and eighty-five severely injured; others were crushed when huge rolls of paper fell through fire-weakened floors into the basement or drowned in the water used to fight the blaze.

Earlier that night, the sound of the rockets that warned of German air raids had caused panic that killed fourteen people in the rush to enter two other shelters. A total of just four German bombers had killed or injured 233 people and created local panic. The thought of a hundred or more bombers battering a city and its frightened inhabitants inspired a vision of cheap and easy victory in the military minds of the day. Mars, the god of war, had grown wings.

The airplane brought war home to the man in the street and his family. French soldiers and civilians search for survivors in the ruins of a village bombed by German aircraft during the conquest of France in 1940.

Chapter I

The Vision of Air Power

THE CONCEPT OF VICTORY THROUGH AIR POWER DID NOT YET REFLECT REALITY during World War I. Although Russia flew multiengine bombers, Italy employed them (some flown by U.S. airmen), and Great Britain created a bomber force to retaliate for the German raids on London, bombers of that era lacked the range, carrying capacity, navigation equipment, and bombsights for sustained and accurate attacks. Dirigibles, which the Germans had used against targets in Great Britain, had one advantage over airplanes—longer range—but they were far more vulnerable because they depended for lift on cells filled with inflammable hydrogen gas. Genuine strategic air warfare—the destruction of industrial targets, population centers, and government facilities to an extent that would force an enemy to yield—remained beyond the abilities of existing aircraft.

Unlike the big bombers, pursuits (the forerunners of modern fighters), observation craft, and light bombers operating in daylight proved deadly over the battlefield, gaining control of the skies, attacking lines of supply and communication, monitoring the movement of friendly and hostile troops, locating targets for artillery, and sometimes strafing enemy trenches and artillery batteries. Tactical aviation, which provided this kind of aerial support for the armies, proved its value during World War I; the strategic bomber remained a weapon of the future.

An Italian airman, Giulio Douhet, ignored the limits of current technology and proposed a battle plane capable of fighting its

LEFT: During World War I, the Germans developed an armored airplane for attacking targets on the ground. Since an Allied tank seems an unlikely victim, even of an armored plane, this picture may well have been staged.

way to a hostile city and destroying it with bombs and poison gas. In *The Command of the Air*, written in 1922, Douhet argued that air attacks on civilians could destroy their will to resist and gain victory without the bloody trench warfare that characterized the conflict just ended. Douhet's argument led inevitably to the conclusion that the air arm of a military force, since it could achieve decisive results on its own, should enjoy coequal status with the army and the navy.

The Evolution of North American Air Power

Within a decade of the publication of Douhet's book, an English translation was making the rounds within the U.S. Army Air Corps (formerly the Army Air Service), but William L. Mitchell, the earliest American advocate of an independent air force, had probably never read it, according to his admirers as well as his critics. A wartime brigadier general, Billy Mitchell inspired loyalty in his disciples and loathing among those who disagreed with him. Mitchell's enemies included the

so-called battleship admirals, Navy men who believed that the fire of the battleships' big guns would decide the outcome of future naval battles. To embarrass the battleship admirals, Mitchell participated in a bombing test off the Virginia capes, bending the rules to make sure that his aircraft sank the anchored ex-German battleship *Ostfriesland*.

The destruction of the U.S. Navy dirigible *Shenandoah*, caught in a thunderstorm during a goodwill tour of the Midwest, gave Mitchell another opportunity to attack the admirals, whom he accused of "incompetency and criminal negligence." This outburst resulted in a trial by court-martial that suspended Mitchell without pay for five years. Shortly after the court's decision, he resigned his commission, though as a civilian he continued to agitate for an independent United States air force, the equal of the U.S. Army and Navy.

Naval aviators also collided with the conservative battleship admirals, but such airmen as Rear Adm. William A. Moffett avoided the confrontational tactics that delighted Mitchell, relying instead on persuasion to influence key civilian politicians and Navy traditionalists. Moreover, naval aviators were not seeking independence; their aim was to become an integral part of a powerful fleet, an objective acceptable to all but the most reactionary of admirals. Consequently, during the 1920s the Department of the Navy sponsored the development of seaplane tenders, aircraft carriers, and even a seagoing mooring mast for dirigibles, thus enabling aviation to accompany the battle fleet.

Although the War Department rejected independence for the air arm, the Army's leadership understood the importance of air support to victory on the battlefield. Over the years, a succession of War Department and congressional actions gradually enhanced the status of military aviation.

In 1926 the U.S. Army Air Service became the Army Air Corps, the organizational equal of combat arms like Infantry and Field Artillery; additional airmen received assignments to the War Department General Staff, and an Assistant Secretary of War for Air represented the interests of military aviation. In 1935 the Air Corps began grouping its bombardment and pursuit aircraft in a General Headquarters Air Force (GHQ Air Force), which trained and would fight as a unit, deploying to meet any threat to the United States. Six years later, the Air Corps became the Army Air Forces, with its Commanding General the equivalent of a Deputy Chief of Staff for air. Ultimately, in 1942, the Commanding General, Army Air Forces, Gen. Henry H. Arnold, became the equal of the commanders of the Army Ground Forces and Army Service Forces. Arnold also served on the Joint Chiefs of Staff along with the Army Chief of Staff, Gen. George C. Marshall,

LEFT, TOP: Adm. William D. Leahy, shown here on the eve of World War II, represented the interests of the United States at Vichy, the capital of Nazi-occupied France, served as wartime Chief of Staff to President Franklin D. Roosevelt, became a member of the American Joint Chiefs of Staff and the Anglo-American Combined Chiefs of Staff, and achieved the five-star rank of Fleet Admiral. LEFT, BOTTOM: Gen. George C. Marshall, the wartime Army Chief of Staff, valued military aviation and, despite his personal reserve, was willing to put up with an occasional practical joke from Gen. Henry H. Arnold, who commanded the Army Air Forces. Marshall granted the air arm a great deal of autonomy within the service in return for Arnold's pledge to postpone the campaign for independence for the air arm until after the war. Both Marshall and Arnold became five-star generals of the Army and served on the Joint and Combined Chiefs of Staff.

RIGHT: The Japanese army's Nakajima Ki-43 fighter, nicknamed Oscar by the Allies, proved comparable in performance to the Japanese navy's more celebrated Mitsubishi Zero fighter. BELOW: The Japanese aircraft carrier *Ryujo*, built under the arms limitation agreements in effect in the early 1930s, displaced 8,000 tons (7,200t). American naval aircraft sank *Ryujo* off the Solomon Islands in August 1942. OPPOSITE: Douglas SBD Dauntless dive-bombers of the U.S. Navy maintain formation during a training flight. The Dauntless bombers, which sank three Japanese aircraft carriers and mortally damaged a fourth at the Battle of Midway, still served Marine Corps airmen as late as the Luzon campaign of 1945, when the bomber helped inspire an irreverent verse: "With the help of God and a few Marines, MacArthur returned to the Philippines."

the Chief of Naval Operations, Adm. Ernest J. King, and the President's Chief of Staff, Adm. William D. Leahy. Thus did Arnold become an equal of Marshall, even though the air arm remained a part of the Army.

In nudging military aviation up the organizational ladder, the War Department devoted a sizable share of its appropriations to the air arm, enabling the force to fly reasonably modern equipment though not to expand to authorized strength. Indeed, Congress rarely voted appropriations to pay for all the men and equipment it authorized. But, besides buying light bombers, attack planes, pursuits, and observation craft useful over the battlefield, the Air Corps had the funds to pursue the dream of strategic bombing, building two huge, experimental bombers, the Boeing XB-15 and Douglas XB-19, and developing the workhorse heavy bombers of World War II, the Boeing B-17 (first flown in 1935) and the Consolidated B-24 (1939).

While the Army air arm increased in numbers, status, and modern equipment, United States naval aviation evolved into a powerful, mobile striking force. Two battle cruisers, canceled because of the Washington Naval Arms Limitation Conference (1921–22), were finished as aircraft carriers USS *Lexington* and *Saratoga*, joining the converted collier USS *Langley*, the Navy's first ship of this type. The Navy added USS *Ranger* in 1934, at 14,500 tons (13,050t), less than half the displacement of the *Lexington* or *Saratoga*.

By 1941, the Navy had also commissioned the aircraft carriers *Enterprise*, *Yorktown*, *Wasp*, and *Hornet*. During this period of growth and expansion, the Navy developed a succession of aircraft culminating in the Grumman F4F fighter, the Douglas SBD dive-bomber, the Douglas TBD torpedo plane, and the Consolidated PBY patrol bomber.

Canada entered the British Commonwealth Air Training Plan in December 1939. Between the spring of the next year, when training began, and the end of the war, almost 132,000 pilots, gunners, radio operators, and navigators trained in Canada, some 55 percent of them Canadian citizens. Canadian airmen flew fighters and transports as well as bombers, but made their greatest and costliest contribution to Bomber Command, in which 9,980 of their number were killed.

RIGHT: Bristol Blenheims, shown here in formation, were typical of the fast medium bombers developed by the British in the 1930s. German fighters had too much speed and firepower for these bombers to operate by day without escort as envisioned in prewar doctrine.

OPPOSITE, TOP: The Vickers Wellington V was a radically modified example of a fast bomber designed before the war for unescorted daylight missions. Driven from the daylight skies, the earlier Wellingtons flew night missions until replaced by four-engine bombers capable of carrying heavier bomb loads, then reverted to training flights and maritime patrol.

OPPOSITE, BOTTOM: This is an early model of the four-engine Avro Lancaster, which evolved from the unsuccessful twin-engine Manchester; together with the Handley Page Halifax and, to a lesser degree, the Short Stirling, the Lancaster deluged German cities with bombs ranging in size from small incendiaries to huge blockbusters.

Developments in Europe and Asia

Great Britain also developed a naval air arm, but the
Royal Navy's aircraft tended to be less formidable than
their United States counterparts and its half-dozen aircraft carriers smaller. The weakness in aircraft may have
stemmed from the fact that, until 1938, the independent
Royal Air Force developed aircraft for the Fleet Air
Arm, trained pilots, and provided maintenance, but
land-based operations and aircraft enjoyed overwhelming priority. Not until 1938 did the Royal Navy assume
full responsibility for its aerial component.

Only Japan developed a carrier air arm comparable
to that of the U.S. Navy. Like its U.S. counterpart, the
Imperial Japanese Navy completed two capital ships, sac-
rificed to the Washington naval limitation negotiations, as

RIGHT: The Supermarine Spitfire XXI was an advanced version of the interceptor that, with the Hawker Hurricane, won the Battle of Britain in 1940. The earlier Spitfire mounted eight .303-caliber machine guns rather than the four 20mm cannons in this model. BELOW: The Boulton-Paul Defiant, its armament of four .303-caliber machine guns concentrated in a power-operated turret behind the pilot, lacked the speed and maneuverability necessary for a daylight fighter and reverted to such utility roles as towing targets for gunnery practice.

large aircraft carriers, *Kaga* and *Akagi*. Until it withdrew from the Washington agreement in 1938, Japan invested the tonnage allotted for aircraft carriers in many smaller ships, like the 8,000-ton (7,200t) *Ryujo* and 15,950-ton (14,355t) *Soryu*, instead of building fewer larger ones.

The Japanese also developed some excellent naval aircraft, varying in size from the four-engine Kawanishi H8K flying boat to the single-engine Mitsubishi A6M Zero fighter, a nimble carrier aircraft with a ferry range that enabled it to shuttle among the former German islands mandated to Japan after World War I. In the vastness of the Pacific, Japan's carrier task forces served as a strategic weapon, capable of cruising a thousand miles or more to attack critical targets, as was demonstrated from Pearl Harbor to Ceylon.

Despite the restrictions imposed by the Treaty of Versailles, which had ended World War I, Germany kept up with the latest developments in military aviation by sending officers for training in the Soviet Union. Sport flying and glider clubs flourished in Germany, as did commercial aviation. As early as 1930 the nation's military leaders, though unwilling to denounce the Versailles agreement, suggested that they might need an air arm of perhaps twenty-two squadrons, exclusively for defensive purposes.

Great Britain's Royal Air Force believed in the effectiveness of the bomber. The service's thinking was shaped by Air Marshal Sir Hugh Trenchard, a veteran of World War I, who in 1928 urged bombing the centers of

production for everything from "boots to battleships." Throughout the 1930s the British air arm, independent of the British army and navy, invested in a series of fast, twin-engine, light and medium bombers, such as the Vickers Wellington—with two-gun, power-operated turrets in the nose and tail—the Handley Page Hampden, and the Bristol Blenheim. In addition, the Royal Air Force began developing the four-engine heavy bombers that would pound Hitler's Germany: the Short Stirling, Handley Page Halifax, and Avro Lancaster.

Despite its commitment to the bomber, during the 1930s the Royal Air Force began to acquire a force of Supermarine Spitfire and Hawker Hurricane interceptors to protect the highly industrialized and densely populated British Isles. The Spitfire and slightly older Hurricane were low-wing, single-place monoplanes mounting, in the latest prewar versions, eight .303-caliber machine guns. More of an experiment than these two fighters was the Boulton-Paul Defiant, which had all its armament—four .303-caliber guns—in a power-operated turret located behind the pilot. The success of these interceptors would depend, however, on a recent development: radio detecting and ranging, or radar.

Throughout the 1920s and into the 1930s, the major powers embraced the airplane as a weapon of both offense and defense, developing ever deadlier types and learning how to use them from land bases or from ships at sea. Before the eyes of the world's airmen danced visions of machines that could vault the trenches, where millions had died during the recent world war, and win a quick victory in an air war by shattering civilian morale or crippling vital industries.

Other innovations, such as radar, code-breaking machines, the jet engine, and atomic energy—in varying stages of theoretical development or actual use by the close of the 1930s—promised to help air power meet the test of a second world war.

Could the airplane perform as its enthusiasts, beginning with Douhet, had claimed, seizing complete control of the skies and gaining victory independently of events on land or at sea? Or were air, sea, and ground forces—given the status of aircraft and ordnance—an interdependent team, each sharing credit for victory or blame for defeat?

Radar

Radar traces its origins to German physicist Heinrich Hertz, who in 1880 discovered that metal reflects radio waves. Great Britain, the United States, Germany, and Japan set to work during the 1920s and 1930s on the military applications of this discovery, and all were successful, though in varying degrees. In radar, transmitters broadcast signals reflected by ships, aircraft, and even features in the terrain; the return could be seen on a cathode ray tube and interpreted by the operator.

As early as 1937, the British demonstrated their leadership in the field by building a series of so-called Chain Home radars to detect bombers approaching from the Continent. Data from these radars and other intelligence on the approach of bomber formations would enable commanders to shift interceptors to meet the threat.

On the eve of war, the Germans became aware of the radar net and sought further intelligence on British radar by sending the elderly dirigible *Graf Zeppelin* to intercept the signals of the Chain Home sets. This slow-flying dirigible, itself easily detected by radar, proved ill-suited for the task.

Fighter controllers in an Essex-class fast carrier direct aerial operations over the China Sea in December 1944. Whether in carriers or picket destroyers, as off Okinawa, radar proved an essential weapon against suicide attack.

Chapter 2

The Approach of War

BY 1939 THREE NATIONS—GERMANY, ITALY, AND JAPAN—SEEMED WILLING, IF not eager, to plunge the world into war, acting independently or in concert.

Japan struck first but limited its ambitions to Asia, seizing Manchuria from China in 1931 and 1932 and during the next two years extending its authority into Mongolia and northern China. To obtain raw materials and markets for manufactured goods, Japan renewed the offensive in China in 1937, capturing the capital, Nanking, and in two years seizing much of the coastline. In December 1937, Japanese aircraft bombed the U.S. gunboat *Panay*, killing two crewmen as well as a civilian passenger. The government of Japan apologized, however, and agreed to pay an indemnity.

Italy, too, engaged in peripheral aggression, far from the continent of Europe. In 1936 the armed forces of Italian dictator Benito Mussolini overwhelmed the ill-equipped forces of Ethiopia and annexed that African kingdom as a colony. Immediately afterward, Italy joined Germany in the Anti-Comintern Pact, a political agreement aimed at containing the Soviet Union, which led in 1939 to the Pact of Steel, a military alliance.

Japan allied itself militarily with Italy and Germany in 1940. Together, Germany, Italy, and Japan constituted the Axis Powers, an extension to the Far East of the Rome-Berlin Axis established by the Anti-Comintern Pact. Singly and in combination, the Axis nations menaced the peace of the world.

The Threat of Hitler's Germany

Despite the restrictions of the Treaty of Versailles, Germany developed an air force designed to fight a war on the European continent. Chosen chancellor in 1933, Adolf Hitler reversed the lingering results of the agreement that had ended World War I within four years. In 1935 Hitler, who wielded the combined

LEFT: Adolf Hitler, Germany's dictator, and (on his left) Hermann Göring, Air Minister and chief of the new Luftwaffe, review a squadron in 1935. The elderly biplanes in the background gave way by 1939 to modern monoplanes like the Junkers Ju 87 dive-bomber and Messerschmitt Me 109 fighter.

powers of chancellor and president and functioned as dictator, unveiled the Luftwaffe, Nazi Germany's new air force.

Armed at first with bombers hurriedly converted from commercial transports and flying biplane fighters, the Luftwaffe soon acquired first-line military aircraft, such as the Junkers Ju 87 dive-bomber, the Heinkel He 111 twin-engine bomber, and the Messerschmitt Bf 109 single-engine fighter and Bf 110 twin-engine fighter. (After Willy Messerschmitt, the designer of these two fighters, formed a company to manufacture them, the wartime prefix Me replaced Bf, which referred to the Bayerische Flugzeugwerke company that had originally built them.)

The Luftwaffe, commanded by Hermann Göring, a fighter ace in World War I, lacked a four-engine heavy bomber, even though German aerial doctrine called for

ABOVE: Wounded from the gunboat USS *Panay* receive emergency care. In December 1937, Japanese aircraft sank *Panay*, clearly marked as a U.S. warship, while it was escorting Standard Oil tankers on China's Yangtze River.
RIGHT: Smoke from fires set by Japanese bombs rises from one of the tankers that *Panay* was escorting.

LEFT, TOP: The Junkers Ju 87 Stuka dive-bomber, shown here with Italian markings, proved deadly early in the war but lacked the speed and defensive firepower to survive against increasingly formidable Allied fighters. Nevertheless, the Stuka supported German forces in every theater of war throughout the conflict. LEFT, BOTTOM: The Heinkel He 111, an effective bomber early in the war, lacked the power-operated turrets necessary to defend against first-line fighters. The plane remained in service, however, and eventually launched flying bombs toward the British Isles.

Adolf Hitler, center, confers with Luftwaffe commander Hermann Göring and another officer at an air show staged by one of the flying clubs absorbed into the Luftwaffe.

attacks on an enemy's industries and governmental structures, targets whose destruction would undermine military efficiency and demoralize the populace. Germany had not yet developed aerial engines efficient enough for a heavy bomber, and developing them from scratch would have absorbed resources and industrial capacity needed for other aircraft better suited to the continental war that Hitler had in mind.

With the Luftwaffe it had built in defiance of the Treaty of Versailles, Germany seemed the likeliest of the three outlaw nations to hurl the thunderbolt of aerial destruction and start another world war. After withdrawing from the League of Nations in 1935, Hitler, the self-styled Führer, or leader, reclaimed the Saar, an industrial area placed under French control to forestall German rearmament, and in 1936 sent troops into the demilitarized Rhineland.

The German dictator tested his air arm in the Spanish Civil War (1936–39), intervening along with Italy's Mussolini to ensure the overthrow of an elected government supported by the Soviet Union. The Soviet air force supplied the Spanish government with excellent fighters, the Polikarpov I-15 biplane and I-16 monoplane, but no heavy bombers. Even though Imperial Russia had experimented with heavy bombers during World War I and the Soviet regime had built massive aircraft for military and propaganda purposes, air power remained tied to the Red Army instead of ranging far ahead to destroy strategic targets.

During the Spanish fighting, the bomber became a symbol of unthinking destruction as the German Condor Legion, under Baron Wolfram von Richthofen, attacked Guernica on market day. Wave after wave of bombers and dive-bombers battered the crowded Basque town, killing as many as 800, wounding twice that number, and inspiring Pablo Picasso's famous painting commemorating that bloody afternoon. According to legend, a German officer saw the gruesome picture and asked Picasso, "Did you do that?" "No," the artist is supposed to have replied. "You did that."

ABOVE: Baron Wolfram von Richthofen commanded the Condor Legion, which destroyed Guernica during the Spanish Civil War and later directed similarly devastating attacks against Warsaw, Poland, and Rotterdam in the Netherlands. LEFT: The Focke Wulf Fw 200, based on a prewar commercial transport, carried troops and cargo and also flew maritime reconnaissance and attack missions against Allied convoys bound for the Soviet port of Murmansk.

LEFT AND BELOW: The twin-engine Lockheed P-38 Lightning, its cockpit shown at left, was designed as an interceptor and had the range and firepower to escort bombers against Germany, but its supercharger tended to fail at high altitudes in the cold skies over northern Europe. The Lightning performed well at lower altitudes especially in the South and Southwest Pacific and North Africa.

President Roosevelt Reacts

German bombing in Spain and Hitler's unopposed conquest of Austria and much of Czechoslovakia in 1938 confirmed the decision by the Royal Air Force to invest in radar-directed interceptors and also to develop heavy bombers. Additionally, Hitler's actions accelerated the growth and modernization of the U.S. Army Air Corps.

Six weeks after the leaders of France and Great Britain acceded at Munich, Germany, to Hitler's dismemberment of Czechoslovakia, President Franklin D. Roosevelt met with Gen. Malin Craig, the Army Chief of Staff; George C. Marshall, the Deputy Chief of Staff, who would succeed Craig in 1939; and General Arnold,

OPPOSITE, TOP: The Bell P-39 Airacobra, designed as an interceptor, had its Allison liquid-cooled engine located behind the pilot to accommodate a 37mm cannon, firing through the propeller hub. An Air Corps decision to eliminate a turbosupercharger from production models limited the P-39 to low- and medium-altitudes, but the plane gave especially effective support to ground troops in the South and Southwest Pacific and, because of Lend-Lease, an agreement which allowed the loan of planes and other matériel among the Allies, to the counterattacking Red Army.

OPPOSITE, BOTTOM: Claire Chennault's American Volunteer Group, the Flying Tigers, flew the Curtiss P-40B in the employ of the government of Nationalist China. Improved models of the P-40 remained in production into 1944, and the plane, intended to support and protect ground forces, formed an important part of Lend-Lease, serving the Allies on almost every battlefront.

the recently appointed Chief of the Air Corps. The Commander in Chief revealed his vision of an Air Corps of 20,000 planes, but since Congress seemed certain to balk at so large an increase, he decided to seek appropriations for only 10,000 airplanes—2,500 trainers and 7,500 combat aircraft. Indeed, the president was more interested in sending a warning to Hitler—which could be done quickly and comparatively cheaply by ordering aircraft—than in attaining a numerical goal.

Arnold later hailed the president's words as a "Magna Carta" for air power, but the general realized at the time that the Roosevelt program stressed aircraft while ignoring manpower. After further discussions, the chief executive reduced the number of new aircraft to 3,000, which with the 2,500 already ordered or on hand, would raise the strength of the Air Corps to 5,500 first-line planes. Of the $300 million voted by Congress for military aviation, $186 million purchased 3,251 new aircraft; the balance paid the cost of recruiting, training, housing, and clothing personnel for an air arm that would eventually double in size to 48,000 by mid-1941.

The expanded Air Corps would fly several new aircraft. The bombers included the four-engine Boeing B-17 Flying Fortress and the twin-engine Douglas B-18, the latter lacking in speed and defensive fire power. A prototype of the four-engine Consolidated B-24 was being built in 1939. The single-engine fighters included the Bell P-39 and the Curtiss P-40, both of which were designed to fight at low and medium altitudes in support of troops on the ground. Only the Lockheed P-38, a radical-looking twin-engine, twin-boom fighter, had superchargers intended for high-altitude operation.

Aware of the powerful isolationist sentiment in the United States, Arnold tried as late as 1939 to present air power, especially the heavy bomber, as a defensive weapon. According to the Chief of the Air Corps, the long-range bombers could deploy anywhere in the Western Hemisphere to attack a hostile beachhead.

Such was the theory; in the event of an actual war, the mission of the big bombers would be offensive—to fight their way to industrial targets in the enemy's heartland and destroy his ability to fight.

Chapter 3

The Struggle Begins

WHILE THE UNITED STATES ARMED, AND GREAT BRITAIN AND FRANCE LOOKED to their defenses, in the spring of 1939 Hitler absorbed the rest of Czechoslovakia and fixed an avaricious eye on Poland. He believed that France and Great Britain, Poland's allies, were too far away to stop a Nazi invasion, but he worried about the Soviet Union, which also coveted Polish territory. Germany therefore negotiated a nonaggression pact with the Soviet Union that, in effect, handed over eastern Poland to the Soviet dictator, Joseph Stalin.

Hitler Attacks

On September 1, 1939, German troops attacked Poland; Me 109 fighters swept the Polish air force from the sky so that light and medium bombers, and the deadly Ju 87B dive-bombers, could destroy military strongpoints and burn the center of Warsaw, the capital city. Von Richthofen, the officer whose Condor Legion bombed Guernica, directed the destruction of Warsaw. Within three weeks the country of Poland no longer existed as a political entity, as Hitler and Stalin divided its territory between them.

German propagandists attributed the victory to mechanized troops supported by an invincible Luftwaffe and warned that the same fate awaited the United Kingdom and France, who went to war on behalf of Poland, and any other nation rash enough to oppose Hitler. In fact, much of the German army had depended on horse-drawn transportation rather than tanks or trucks, and the Luftwaffe destroyed only fifty more Polish aircraft than it lost to fighters, antiaircraft fire, and accidents.

LEFT: Smoke billows over London as the result of a German daylight raid on September 7, 1940. Although the Luftwaffe inflicted heavy damage on the London docks, the Hurricanes and Spitfires of Fighter Command forced the enemy to attack by night, relying on radio beams that reduced bombing accuracy.

World War II began in September 1939 when Hitler and Stalin divided Poland between their countries. Germany had already absorbed Austria and Czechoslovakia. France and Great Britain responded by declaring war on Germany but could not move decisively enough to save the Poles. In the spring of 1940, Hitler overran Denmark, Norway, the Netherlands, Belgium, and France.

In the meantime, Stalin accepted Hitler's assurances of friendship and invaded Finland, seizing territory to preempt a supposed threat to the Soviet Union's northwestern territory.

Italy stayed neutral at first. Not until Germany had clearly defeated France did Mussolini join the conflict as Hitler's ally. North Africa, where Italy had colonies, became the principal theater of operations for Italian forces.

Air power contributed to Hitler's victories in Europe, supporting the advancing armies and in the process leveling Warsaw and Rotterdam. London and other British cities suffered grave damage from aerial bombardment but survived, and the Germans never gained the control of the skies necessary for an invasion.

Hitler overran the Balkans, Greece, and Crete; took over the war in North Africa from the Italians; and in June 1941 launched a surprise attack on the Soviet Union.

Europe and North Africa at the Outbreak of World War II

The swift victory over Poland reinforced the self-conceit of the Nazi hierarchy. The aircraft that had overcome the poorly equipped Polish air arm, destroyed towns, and strafed troops and road traffic seemed to them more than adequate for a war against France and Great Britain. The Luftwaffe continued to rely on comparatively short-range fighters and light and medium bombers defended by hand-operated machine guns. The only long-range, four-engine aircraft readily available was the Focke Wulf Fw 200 Kondor, a maritime reconnaissance craft based on a prewar transport.

Moreover, Germany failed to increase aircraft production to meet the demands of a long war. During all of 1939, German industry produced a thousand more aircraft than British factories, but by December Great Britain would take the lead in monthly output.

The Fighting in the West
Although the British, French, and German governments designated bomb shelters, issued gas masks, and set up

The German conquerors of Poland pass in review before Adolf Hitler during the Führer's visit to heavily bombed Warsaw. Nazi propagandists cited the rapid conquest as proof of German invincibility.

German troops set up antiaircraft batteries as they consolidate their grip on Poland. While Hitler attacked from the west, Soviet troops overran the eastern part of the country.

Einstein's Letter

Hitler's acquisition of Czechoslovakia and its uranium mines alarmed several physicists who had recently fled Europe and were familiar with the research in nuclear energy under way at Berlin's Kaiser Wilhelm Institute.

Two knowledgeable scientists warned the U.S. Navy but got no reaction. The group therefore arranged a direct approach to President Roosevelt from the United States' best-known scientist, Nobel laureate Albert Einstein, himself a refugee from Nazi Germany. Einstein's carefully reasoned letter, dated August 2, 1939, and an accompanying memorandum by another refugee physicist, Leo Szilard, set in motion the development of the atomic bomb. No responsible politician could ignore the judgment of so famous a scientist as Einstein that an atomic bomb was indeed feasible.

antiaircraft batteries, the air war started slowly, consisting in 1939 of inconclusive attacks on ports and shipping. The twin-engine British bombers, of which so much had been expected, lacked the speed and firepower to survive against the German Me 109s, which mounted one or two 20mm cannon and a pair of machine guns. For example, the Wellington, despite its power turrets fore and aft, had only hand-operated guns to defend against attacks from the beam.

As though aware of the vulnerability of their own cities, the combatants seemed reluctant to launch an all-out air campaign. The lull in the air coincided with stalemate on the ground. Blitzkrieg, or lightning war, as the Germans described the campaign against Poland, gave way to *sitzkrieg*, a war of sitting.

Nazi Germany shattered the quiet in April 1940, attacking two neutral nations, Denmark and Norway. Danish resistance collapsed quickly, providing airfields to support the conquest of Norway, but the Norwegians resisted, despite the treasonous activity of a band of Nazi sympathizers led by Minister of War Vidkun Quisling. German paratroops seized important airfields,

The Fairey Battle, a prewar light bomber, had become obsolete when the war began, as demonstrated by the gallant but futile attack on the many German forces swarming across the Meuse River in 1940.

where trimotor Junkers Ju 52 transports disgorged reinforcements, and Hitler's navy landed other troops by sea. The operation cost the Germans the cruiser *Konigsberg,* sunk by a Blackburn Skua dive-bomber from the carrier HMS *Ark Royal* on April 10. Norwegian forces held out long enough for the Allies to land expeditionary forces at three points on the coast, but only at Narvik, in the far north, could the troops carve out a beachhead.

As the British, French, and Polish force clung to the Narvik outpost, on May 10 Hitler invaded the neutral Netherlands, using the Luftwaffe to land assault troops as it had in Norway. Dutch pilots fought back, however, shooting down a number of troop-laden Ju 52s before Me 109s could seize control of the skies. A savage aerial bombardment of central Rotterdam, comparable to the attack on Warsaw, forced the Dutch to surrender.

In attacking Belgium, another neutral, German assault troops landed from gliders and used shaped explosive charges to penetrate the walls of key forts guarding the Belgian border. After silencing the forts,

the attacking Germans trapped the French troops that had entered Belgium to blunt the offensive. The main German thrust, however, erupted from the Ardennes, and German columns crossed the Meuse River at Dinant and Sedan.

The British reacted by sending some seventy Fairey Battle single-engine light bombers against the crossings, but mobile antiaircraft guns broke up the attack, shooting down more than half of the planes. After the German breakthrough, Winston Churchill refused to risk Hurricane fighters needed for the defense of the British Isles by sending them to airfields in France in what he considered a hopeless attempt to turn defeat into victory.

A combination of indecision and exhaustion halted German forces before they could overrun the rapidly shrinking Allied beachhead in Belgium, and almost 340,000 British and French soldiers escaped through the port of Dunkirk, in France, though they left behind much of their heavy equipment. The withdrawal from Dunkirk ended on June 4, and four days later the Narvik expedition boarded ships and set sail for the British Isles.

RIGHT: A Spitfire roars past a Heinkel He 111 in a photo taken from the cockpit of the German bomber. BELOW: Bombs dropped from a Bristol Blenheim explode during a daylight attack on port facilities at Rotterdam in the Nazi-occupied Netherlands.

On June 8, the aircraft carrier HMS *Glorious*, escorted by two destroyers as it withdrew from Norwegian waters, encountered the German battle cruisers *Gneisenau* and *Scharnhorst*, which sank all three British ships. Italy entered the war on June 10 as an ally of Germany, and France signed an armistice twelve days later.

Great Britain, along with its commonwealth and the governments-in-exile from Nazi-occupied Europe, continued the fight. Hitler's enemies would receive material aid from the United States, which President Roosevelt hoped to convert into an arsenal of democracy. On May 16, with German forces advancing west of the Meuse, the President looked to his country's defense, asking Congress for a force of 50,000 planes divided among the Army Air Forces, Navy, and Marine Corps.

The Army Air Forces alone would expand to 200,000 officers and men and receive 11,000 new aircraft. The total of 50,000 planes remained an elusive goal, however; as late as November 1940, U.S. factories were delivering only 50 planes per week. If the United States were to fulfill Roosevelt's dream of an arsenal supplying Hitler's enemies, new factories would have to be built at government expense, production techniques improved, profits assured, and a rational basis established for dividing production between Britain and the United States.

The Battle of Britain

While Roosevelt took steps toward providing Great Britain with what he characterized as all aid short of war, Hitler prepared to conquer the British Isles before U.S. aid could make a difference. Hermann Göring, who headed both the Luftwaffe and the air ministry, assured the Führer that he could seize control of the skies, enabling an invasion armada to defy the Royal Air Force and cross the English Channel.

Pilots sprint to their Hawker Hurricane fighters as German bombers approach from occupied Europe. Later models of the Hurricane, some of them armed with 40mm guns, specialized in supporting troops.

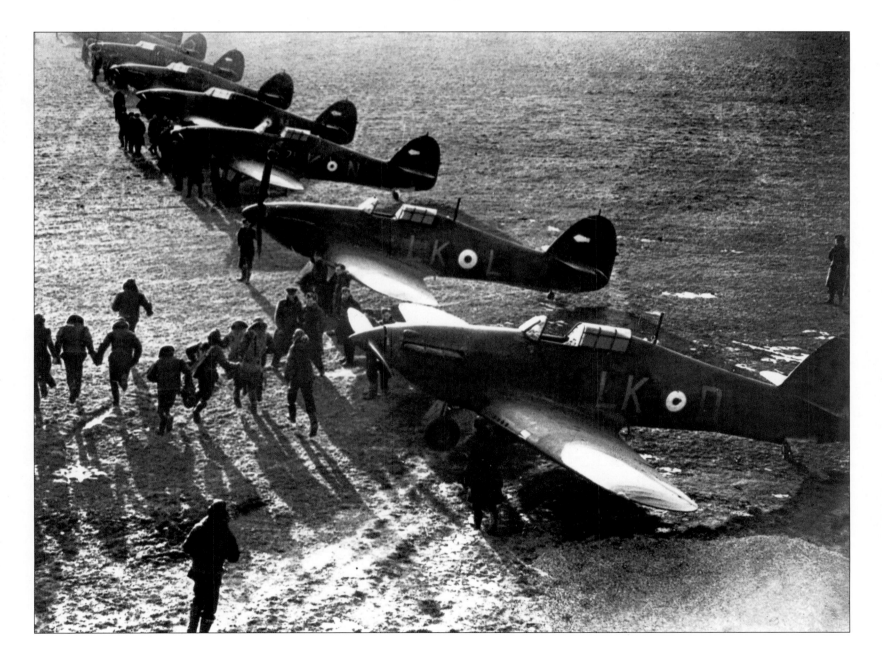

Ultra Intelligence

The Luftwaffe suffered the consequences of Britain's ability to read German communications encrypted on the Enigma machine and to disseminate the contents as Ultra, a highly secret category of intelligence.

Enigma's combination of keyboard, plugs, rotors, and relays automatically encrypted a message as it was typed, and decryption occurred automatically since the receiving machine would have the same daily setting as the sender. To handle Enigma's hundreds of thousands of permutations, cryptanalysts at the Government Code and Cipher School at Bletchley Park, a Victorian mansion not far from London, used primitive computers that mimicked Enigma to attack the encrypted text swiftly and tirelessly. If operational messages were broken in time, Royal Air Force Fighter Command could use Ultra, supported by radar sightings and other information, to determine the size, target, and timing of a German raid and respond accordingly.

ABOVE: The dome of St. Paul's Cathedral in London stands defiantly against the smoke and flames caused by a German incendiary raid on December 29, 1940. RIGHT: The Dornier Do 17 Flying Pencil revealed during the Battle of Britain that its hand-operated light machine guns could not enable it to bomb by daylight without a fighter escort.

At this critical time, however, the shortcomings of the Luftwaffe surfaced with a vengeance. The fast, maneuverable Me 109 lacked the endurance for sustained combat over the British Isles, and the Me 110 could not maneuver with the faster Hurricanes and Spitfires. Without an effective fighter escort, German light and medium bombers and dive-bombers could not duplicate the deadly work they had accomplished by daylight on the continent of Europe. Air defenses stronger than any yet encountered inflicted severe losses on the bomber formations, and German aircrews who parachuted into Britain became prisoners of war. To accelerate the rate of attrition, Churchill directed British pilots to destroy unarmed German seaplanes, marked with the red cross, that tried to rescue aviators downed at sea. Additionally, the first Canadian fighter squadron had arrived in time to help fight the Battle of Britain.

Air Marshal Sir Hugh Dowding, who directed Fighter Command, relied on code-breaking for insights into German intentions that enabled him to dispatch force enough to deal with the day's threat while retaining a reserve for any possible emergency. Some of his subordinates, not knowing about Ultra (see sidebar, page 38), complained bitterly that he was gambling the nation's future, apparently relying on radar and his own instincts, instead of meeting each raid with overwhelming force. Despite the complaints about Dowding's leadership, British pilots fought gallantly.

Indeed, one of Dowding's most bitter critics, Squadron Leader Douglas R.S. Bader—who flew with artificial legs as the result of a prewar crash—claimed that the three squadrons temporarily entrusted to him destroyed more than a hundred German aircraft during a single week in September, at the cost of fourteen fighters. Although claims by all pilots tended to be exaggerated, the success of Bader's squadrons convinced him that Dowding erred in trying to meet each threat with just enough force; the more Spitfires and Hurricanes that tangled with the Luftwaffe, the greater the German losses would be, he thought.

Bader's aggressive style occasionally verged on insubordination, for his squadrons sometimes abandoned their assigned areas and went hunting on their own, suddenly popping up on radar screens and startling the

LEFT: The Messerschmitt Me 110 twin-engine fighter, the instrument panel of which is shown here, lacked the speed and maneuverability needed for daytime operations but became a successful night fighter when fitted with airborne radar. BELOW: Air Marshal Sir Hugh Dowding won the Battle of Britain, but he could not reveal the secret intelligence that contributed to the victory and was replaced by those who criticized his tactics.

controllers who assumed at least briefly that these were the enemy. Forbidden to reveal the existence of Ultra, Dowding could not answer Bader and the other critics, who eventually rallied enough political support to replace him, though not until after he had won the Battle of Britain. Dissatisfied though he was, Bader helped gain the victory; by August 1941, when he was shot down over France and captured, he had downed twenty-two Luftwaffe aircraft.

Other British fighter pilots shared Bader's courage, though not his impatience with discipline. Adolph G. "Sailor" Malan, a South African, downed thirty-two aircraft during the war, impressing his fellow pilots as early as the Battle of Britain with his cool professionalism. Legend has it that he once calmly changed a lightbulb in his optical gun sight during an air battle.

Posing here with his battle-damaged Hurricane, Douglas R.S. Bader advocated intercepting German raids with an overwhelming number of fighters and, since he knew nothing of Ultra, had no sympathy for Air Marshal Sir Hugh Dowding's policy of meeting each threat with just enough fighters, while retaining a reserve for emergencies. Bader's determination in learning to fly fighters, despite his artificial legs, and his undeniable skill and courage lent force to the successful campaign to have Dowding removed as head of Fighter Command.

Göring made several errors in fighting the Battle of Britain. He failed to knock out the Chain Home radars, the destruction of which should have been first priority. The Luftwaffe also broke off its successful attacks on Dowding's airfields, resuming instead a war of attrition in the skies as it concentrated on urban targets and the destruction of civilian morale. Göring, however, could not destroy more British airplanes than he lost. On August 13, *Adlertag*, or Eagle Day, he dispatched almost 1,500 fighters and bombers, losing more than three times as many aircraft as the British, along with their crews.

By mid-September Ultra revealed that Hitler had postponed indefinitely the invasion of the British Isles, but hit-and-run raids continued into October—as on October 15, when high-flying Me 109s scattered bombs that hit Waterloo Station. The declining intensity of the aerial fighting over the British Isles confirmed that Dowding had defeated Göring. The inability of German fighters to protect bombers in daylight forced the Luftwaffe to bomb by night with the aid of radio beams. Despite spectacular fires, as at London and Coventry, the night raids neither destroyed British morale nor crippled the nation's industries. Indeed, British aircraft production increased during the summer and autumn of 1940.

Churchill paid eloquent tribute to Dowding's triumphant fliers, declaring, "Never in the field of human conflict was so much owed by so many to so few." Appropriately the only British fighter pilot to receive the Victoria Cross, the nation's highest award for valor, earned his decoration in the Battle of Britain. On August 16, Flight Lieutenant James Nicolson continued to attack an Me 110, even though flames had erupted in his cockpit, painfully burning his hands and face. Not until he had destroyed the Messerschmitt did he parachute from his doomed Hurricane. Defense forces on the ground mistook him and another British pilot, who had also taken to his parachute, for German paratroopers and opened fire, swiftly killing the other airman and wounding Nicolson.

Hitler Turns East

His plan for conquering Britain frustrated by Fighter Command, Hitler directed his energies elsewhere. He sent German troops to fight alongside his Italian allies in North Africa, went to the aid of Italian forces bogged down in Greece, and overran Yugoslavia.

On May 20, 1941, after the conquest of Greece, Germany launched a successful airborne operation, employing transports and gliders to land between 20,000 and 30,000 troops, who conquered the island of Crete.

Although the Luftwaffe controlled the skies, the Royal Navy succeeded in evacuating some 18,000 of Crete's defenders—slightly more than were killed, wounded, or captured—but the fleet lost three cruisers and six destroyers sunk by air attack, along with an aircraft carrier, three battleships, six cruisers, and seven destroyers damaged. The Royal Air Force lost twenty-three fighters and an equal number of bombers. German casualties totaled 6,000; never again would Germany attempt so ambitious an airborne assault.

Hitler's successes inspired the Roosevelt administration to overhaul its machinery for supervising war production. Robert M. Lovett, a naval aviator in World War I, became Secretary of War for Air in November 1940, specializing in aircraft production. Roosevelt also established a National Defense Advisory Commission, redesignated the Office of Production Management in 1941 and ultimately the War Production Board. Thanks in part to these reforms, the number of military and naval aircraft turned out by American factories dramatically increased from 2,141 in 1939 to 19,000 in 1941.

These airplanes, however, had to be shared with he nations actually fighting Hitler. In March 1941, President Roosevelt persuaded Congress to pass the Lend-Lease Act, which authorized the loan of war material, requiring only that any surviving equipment be returned when the conflict ended. In this way, Great Britain could acquire U.S. weapons without having to buy them. During the war, the United Kingdom and the British Commonwealth received 26,000 aircraft through Lend-Lease. China, a victim of Japanese aggression, soon became eligible as well and received 1,400 planes. The Soviet Union also qualified after Hitler invaded and was provided 11,450 aircraft.

In defiance of their nonaggression pact, on June 22, 1941, Germany attacked the Soviet Union. Hitler and his generals planned to duplicate their victories over Poland and France, despite this latest enemy's vast territory, huge population, industrial base, and natural resources.

An Anglo-American Strategic Concept

Over the years, American planners had maintained a series of color-coded war plans, each aimed at a specific nation, such as Orange for Japan. The emergence of the Axis powers revealed a need to combine at least some of the color plans in a new series nicknamed Rainbow. By the summer of 1941, the likeliest of the new plans was Rainbow 5, which envisioned a war wherein the United States was allied with the British Commonwealth against Germany, Italy, and Japan. The strategy called for first defeating Germany, which seemed the strongest Axis power.

The priorities of Rainbow 5 soon became Anglo-American strategy. In late January 1941, American and British planners began a series of conversations in Washington, D.C., during which they discussed the implications of an Anglo-American war against the Axis. Although the officers could not make binding commitments, they agreed in principle that the defeat of Hitler should take precedence.

In defeating Nazi Germany, American bombers would operate from the British Isles under American command, though collaborating with the Royal Air Force. The lower-level discussions at Washington led to a meeting in August between Churchill and Roosevelt at Placentia Bay, Newfoundland, which confirmed the policy of Germany first.

The Consolidated B-24 Liberator, along with the Boeing B-17 Flying Fortress, helped carry out the Allied strategy of defeating Hitler first, conducting missions against such distant targets as Ploesti, Romania, in 1943. Because of its long range, the Liberator proved especially useful for antisubmarine patrol and, later, for bombing outlying Japanese bases in the Pacific Ocean Areas.

The B-17s that flew their first missions against Germany early in 1943 proved vulnerable to head-on attack. The addition of a "chin" turret and "cheek" guns increased firepower in the front.

By striking hard, moving swiftly, and using air power in close cooperation with the ground forces, the invaders proposed to gain victory before the Soviet Union could marshal its strength.

Ultra revealed Hitler's intentions, however, and Churchill, without describing his source, passed the information on to Stalin, who dismissed it as propaganda designed to sour relations between the Soviet Union and Germany.

Although the actual attack by Germany caught Stalin by surprise, he soon recovered. The Soviet Union not only began a fighting retreat that lured the attackers to the very gates of Moscow but also transplanted entire factories eastward beyond reach of the advancing Germans. The factories thus deployed were soon producing new aircraft that matched the German types in quality and surpassed them in numbers.

An American Plan for Aerial Victory

Hitler's attack on the Soviet Union caused President Roosevelt to call upon the Army and Navy to estimate the overall production requirements for defeating the Axis. The Air War Plans Division of the Army Air Forces received orders to prepare an annex to the Army's response. The air annex—Air War Plans Division/1, or AWPD/1—came to the conclusion that to destroy Hitler's Germany first and then Japan would require an Army air arm of two million men, 135,000 of them pilots.

Against Germany, the Army Air Forces would operate 2,000 fighters and 1,060 medium bombers, plus 3,740 B-17s, B-24s, and yet-to-be-developed Boeing B-29s, attacking from bases in Egypt and the British Isles. A force of intercontinental bombers, which appeared after the war as the Convair B-36, would bomb

Germany from bases in the United States. While the bomber force grew to 7,500 aircraft, the interim force of 3,740 bombers would begin an assault on Germany's aircraft industry, its power grid, its transportation system, and its oil industry. Not until these vital targets had been destroyed would air power turn against the populace, attempting to crush civilian morale.

The plan to bomb Germany into submission ignored the experience of both the Luftwaffe and the Royal Air Force, which had shown that successful daylight bombing required a fighter escort. Army Air Forces planners believed that U.S. bomber formations could fight their way to industrial targets by day and bomb accurately in clear weather, using optical sights to drop 90 percent of their bombs within 1,250 feet (381m) of the aiming point. Unfortunately, weather would prove uncooperative, enemy interceptors and antiaircraft fire would affect accuracy, and even with radar, 90 percent of U.S. bombs exploded within a mile (1.6km) of the target, an area more than four times as large as planners had assumed.

Moreover, building bombers and training crews would take time, but organizing and arming massive ground forces could take even longer, so that for a time the only American weapon available to attack Germany might well be air power.

The British Improve Night Bombing

Even as the Army Air Forces endorsed daylight bombing, during 1941 the Royal Air Force made some embarrassing discoveries about the effectiveness of its night-bombing campaign.

A study of 650 aerial photographs, taken between June 2 and July 25, of 100 separate raids on 28 different targets revealed that only one third of the bombers had dumped their loads within 5 miles (8km) of their targets. Against the Ruhr, industrial haze, smoke screens, and antiaircraft fire prevented the bombers from achieving even minimal accuracy. The inability to find and destroy individual factories caused a shift to area bombing—aiming for the center of the urban mass. Air Marshal Sir Arthur Harris, who headed Bomber Command, described the results as "dehousing," a euphemism for

killing, maiming, or driving from their homes war-workers and their families, who seemed easier targets than factories or machinery.

The British tried to make the nighttime area bombing as deadly as possible, at first by following the German example and employing radio beacons and, beginning in 1943, by using airborne radar. To take full advantage of these navigation aids, Bomber Command used a pathfinder force, organized, trained, and led by an Australian officer, Donald C. T. Bennett, which dropped incendiary bombs or flares to mark the center of a city for the bomber stream that followed.

Danger in the Orient

Although Germany seemed the most dangerous of the Axis partners, Japan sought to take advantage of Hitler's successes, even as it continued its war against China.

A waist gunner of a B-17 functioned in a space so confined that he could not wear a parachute. White safety tape tied the gunner to his chute, enabling him to retrieve it and snap it in place before jumping from the bomber.

Of the officers who played a critical role in the air war against Hitler, three are (left to right) Gen. Henry H. Arnold, Commanding General, Army Air Forces; Air Chief Marshal Sir Arthur Harris, Commander in Chief, Royal Air Force Bomber Command; and Lt. Gen. Ira Eaker, commander of VIII Bomber Command and Eighth Air Force during 1942 and 1943.

the summer of 1941 in the freezing of Japanese assets in the United States. This decision denied Japan access to funds it might have used to buy oil for its war machine.

Because the Philippines posed a potential threat to a Japanese invasion fleet bound for Southeast Asia or the Netherlands East Indies, the Roosevelt administration strengthened the defenses of the islands. General Douglas MacArthur, a retired Army Chief of Staff, assumed command of the Philippine military establishment and began building up the armed forces to defend the islands. Encouraged by MacArthur's progress and aware of Japan's ambitions, the War Department recalled the general to active duty, sent him a modest number of reinforcements, and placed him in command of all the United States troops in the islands, including the Philippine Army.

The reinforcements included Boeing B-17 bombers for the Air Forces, U.S. Army Forces in the Far East, redesignated the Far East Air Forces in November 1941. Secretary of War Henry L. Stimson believed that comparatively few Flying Fortresses could deter further Japanese aggression in the Far East. On September 5, 1941, a flight of nine B-17Ds took off from Hickam Field, Hawaii, on a course that took them to Midway and Wake Islands, New Guinea, and Australia; the bombers landed at Clark Field, near Manila on the island of Luzon, on September 26 in a driving rain.

Between Wake Island and New Guinea, while crossing the Caroline Islands, one of the Japanese Mandates, the formation climbed to 26,000 feet (7900m), an altitude believed to be beyond the reach of Japanese fighters. Another twenty-six B-17s reached the Philippines in November, after detouring south of the Carolines by way of Christmas Island, Canton Island, the Fiji group, New Caledonia, and Australia. A third group of fourteen Flying Fortresses—new D models like others sent to the far Pacific—was preparing on December 6, 1941, to begin its deployment, arriving at Hickam Field on the next morning.

Maj. Gen. Lewis H. Brereton, who took over the Far East Air Forces in November 1941, had amassed a hundred modern P-40s, along with sixty-eight obsolete fighters, to protect the bombers gathering in the Philippines. A radar site at Iba Field on Luzon would

In 1940, after the fall of France, the Japanese obtained the use of ports and airfields in French Indochina, gaining access to raw materials needed for the war in China and outflanking the Philippines, a United States possession. Exploitation of the French colony gave way in July 1941 to occupation, a further step toward acquiring the oil of the Netherlands East Indies, a colony of another of Hitler's victims, and the resources of the British colonies of Malaya and Burma.

President Roosevelt could not ignore the threat from Japan. As a warning, in April 1940 he shifted the Pacific Fleet from San Pedro, California, to Pearl Harbor, Hawaii. When Japan ignored this gesture, the administration invoked economic sanctions that culminated in warn the fighter squadrons of a Japanese air attack from Formosa (now Taiwan) to the north. Brereton might hold his B-17s at bases on Mindanao, beyond range of the Japanese bombers, and at the onset of war deploy them through Clark Field to attack the Japanese bases on Formosa. In early December, however, the bomber force remained evenly divided between Del Monte on Mindanao and Clark Field, Luzon.

The Hawaiian Air Force, commanded since November 1940 by Maj. Gen. Frederick L. Martin, had grown in strength as U.S. Navy aircraft carriers began delivering P-40 fighters and second-line Curtiss P-36s. In all, Martin had ninety-nine P-40s, thirty-nine P-36s, and fourteen obsolete Boeing P-26s. His bomber force consisted of a dozen B-17s, thirty-three obsolete B-18s, and twelve new Douglas A-20 attack planes. The general did not have enough bombers to participate with Navy patrol planes in a joint search plan that would have provided 360-degree coverage of the seaward approaches to the island of Oahu. Martin hoped to reduce the vulnerability of his aircraft by dispersing them among newly built auxiliary fields throughout the Hawaiian chain, but land proved too costly.

In Hawaii, as in the Philippines, the Army Air Forces lacked the strength for successful defense; instead of affording protection, air power merely presented a tempting target for surprise attack. The situation in Hawaii was further complicated by a warning, based on intercepted and decoded Japanese diplomatic messages, to beware of sabotage. Because of this alert, Martin concentrated his planes at the main airfields and parked them in neat rows that could be easily guarded.

Japan faced a strategic dilemma. The nation had to have the oil of the Netherlands East Indies to fight a war, but it dared not grab for this prize while United States warships could sortie from Pearl Harbor. The Imperial Japanese Navy would have to invest some of its existing oil reserves in operations to destroy, or at least neutralize, the Pacific Fleet.

Adm. Isoroku Yamamoto devised a plan for a surprise attack on Pearl Harbor that, if successful, would clear the way for the conquest of the Philippines, Malaya, Burma, and the Netherlands East Indies. Japanese strategy, however, rested more on hopeful

assumptions than on hard facts: Japan would seize a perimeter, exploit its resources, fortify it, and hold it until the potentially stronger United States lost heart and accepted Japanese domination of the western Pacific.

Unlike some of his fellow officers, Yamamoto realized the struggle would be difficult, with victory by no means certain. He expected to "run wild for the first six months or a year," but he had "utterly no confidence for the second and third year."

Adm. Isoroku Yamamoto (left) inspired the attack on Pearl Harbor. Having lived in the United States as a naval attaché and a student, he had no illusions of an easy war against a nation with vast natural resources and production capacity.

Chapter 4

The World at War

ON THE MORNING OF SUNDAY, DECEMBER 7, 1941, A PAIR OF U.S. ARMY
radar operators, practicing during nonduty hours, detected a large number of aircraft approaching
the Hawaiian island of Oahu. They assumed these were United States planes, and no one stood by
at the control center to suggest otherwise. The approaching formation consisted, however, of
Japanese carrier aircraft executing Adm. Yamamoto's bold plan to cripple the Pacific Fleet at the
onset of war with the United States.

Japan's Victories

At 7:55 A.M., the first of two attacking waves, about forty-five minutes apart, pounced on the
anchored warships of the Pacific Fleet and the air, naval, and military installations on the island of Oahu.

This staggering blow, planned by Yamamoto and delivered by
Vice Adm. Chuichi Nagumo, surprised the Americans, sinking or
damaging eight battleships and ten lesser warships, although the
U.S. aircraft carriers remained at sea that morning and escaped
damage. Besides neutralizing the battle fleet, the attack killed
2,403 Americans and wounded 1,178, at a cost to the carrier force
of 29 airplanes lost and 55 crewmen killed. The Japanese also
damaged airfields and other installations—for example, destroying
more than a hundred of General Martin's Army airplanes, almost

LEFT: Smoke from Japanese
bombs and torpedoes rises
from Battleship Row, off Ford
Island at Pearl Harbor, on
the morning of December 7,
1941. The surprise attack
sank two of the battleships
at anchor here, damaged the
other five, and damaged yet
another battleship in drydock.

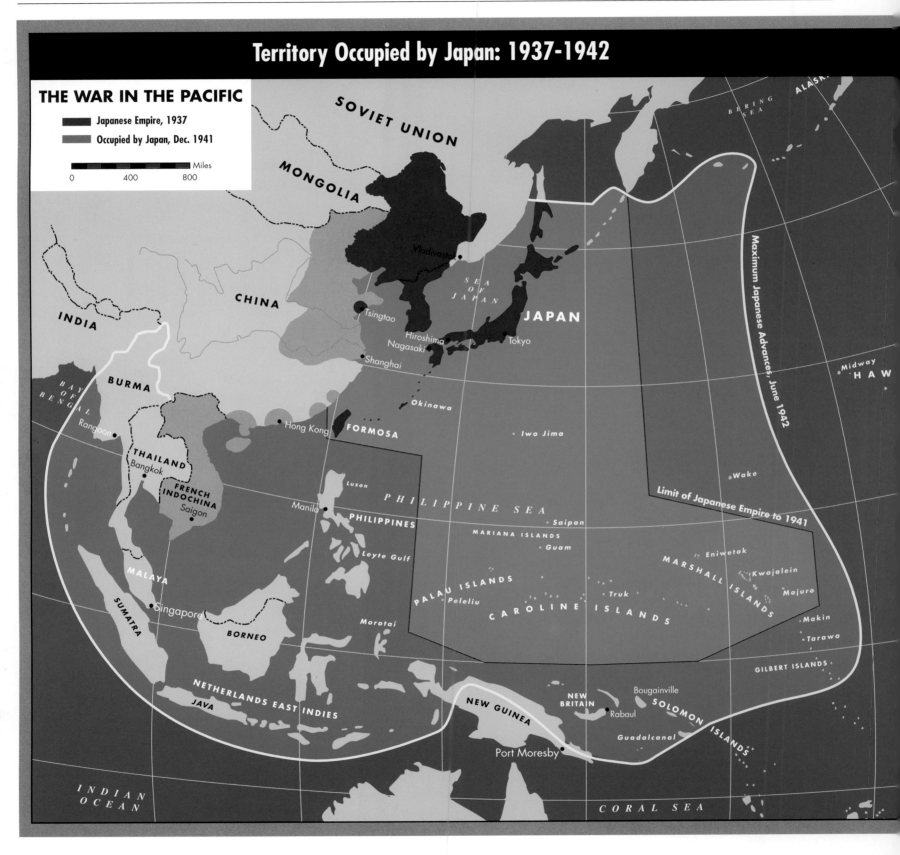

Territory Occupied by Japan: 1937-1942

THE WAR IN THE PACIFIC

- Japanese Empire, 1937
- Occupied by Japan, Dec. 1941

Miles
0   400   800

SOVIET UNION

MONGOLIA

CHINA

INDIA

BURMA

Rangoon

THAILAND
Bangkok

FRENCH
INDOCHINA
Saigon

BAY
OF
BENGAL

MALAYA

SUMATRA

Singapore

BORNEO

JAVA

NETHERLANDS EAST INDIES

INDIAN
OCEAN

Vladivostok

Tsingtao

Hiroshima
Nagasaki

Shanghai

Hong Kong

FORMOSA

Okinawa

SEA
OF
JAPAN

JAPAN

Tokyo

Iwo Jima

Luzon

Manila

PHILIPPINES

Leyte Gulf

PHILIPPINE SEA

Saipan

MARIANA ISLANDS

Guam

PALAU ISLANDS

Peleliu

Truk

CAROLINE ISLANDS

Morotai

NEW GUINEA

Port Moresby

CORAL SEA

NEW
BRITAIN

Rabaul

Bougainville

Guadalcanal

SOLOMON ISLANDS

BERING
SEA

ALASKA

Maximum Japanese Advances, June 1942

Midway

HAW

Wake

Limit of Japanese Empire to 1941

Eniwetok

Kwajalein

MARSHALL ISLANDS

Majuro

Makin

Tarawa

GILBERT ISLANDS

LEFT: As a reward for joining the Allies in World War I, Japan received a League of Nations mandate over the former German colonies in the central Pacific, thus acquiring an empire embracing the Mariana Islands (except for U.S.-held Guam), the Marshalls, and the Carolines. The war in China and the occupation of French Indochina rounded out the territory Japan ruled at the time of the attack on Pearl Harbor.

As Adm. Yamamoto had predicted, Japan "ran wild" at the outset, capturing the Philippines, the Gilbert and Solomon Islands, the Netherlands East Indies, and Burma, gaining a foothold in New Guinea, and threatening India. In the summer of 1942, the tidal wave of Japanese conquests crested with a lodgement in the Aleutians and then began to recede.

all of them on the ground—but the attackers failed to destroy the oil storage tanks on which the U.S. naval operations depended.

A few of General Martin's fighter pilots succeeded in taking off in time to do battle with the second wave. Second Lts. Kenneth Taylor, Harry W. Brown, Philip M. Rasmussen, and George S. Welch claimed the destruction of nine Japanese planes, and First Lt. John Dains may have downed another before being shot down and killed by friendly antiaircraft fire.

Others besides Dains encountered friendly fire over Pearl Harbor. The carrier *Enterprise*, returning after delivering fighters to Wake Island, dispatched nineteen SBD dive-bombers to the airfield at Ford Island, near the center of Pearl Harbor, where they arrived during the Japanese attack. American antiaircraft fire downed one of the planes from *Enterprise*, but the two-man crew survived; enemy fighters destroyed four other dive-bombers, killing all on board.

In addition to the U.S. Navy planes, twelve B-17s had taken off from California and arrived during the

ABOVE: Japanese crewmen wave their encouragement as a bomber in the first wave starts down the deck to attack Pearl Harbor.

The battleship USS *Arizona*, shattered by explosions, sinks to the bottom of Pearl Harbor. A torpedo apparently hit the ship moments before an aerial bomb, probably a fourteen-inch (36cm) armor-piercing shell fitted with fins, detonated the main powder magazine.

attack; two others had turned back with mechanical problems. The arriving bombers carried no ammunition in order to save weight for additional fuel, and the guns were stored amidships to keep the bombers in trim. While Japanese fighters swarmed around the defenseless bombers, antiaircraft guns blazed away, but, incredibly, all the Flying Fortresses made successful landings, one on the rolling greens of a golf course. Eleven survived to fly again, thereby reinforcing the surviving remnants of Martin's Hawaiian Air Force.

Beyond the international date line, in the Philippines, where it was December 8, Japanese

bombers based on Formosa were to attack the Philippines as the carrier strike force hit Pearl Harbor, but fog over Formosa kept the enemy on the ground until MacArthur's headquarters had received word of the attack on Oahu.

All the American principals—MacArthur himself; his chief of staff, Maj. Gen. Richard K. Sutherland; and Gen. Brereton of the Far East Air Forces—later offered conflicting explanations of what happened. Whatever the truth, Japanese bombers took off after the fog had burned away, caught seventeen Flying Fortresses on the ground at Clark Field as they were taking on bombs and fuel to attack Formosa, and destroyed them all. The P-40s assigned to protect the bombers were preparing to take off when the Japanese appeared, and only three of them got into the air, destroying no more than four enemy aircraft. The day's attacks claimed roughly half of Brereton's air force.

The surviving eighteen B-17s in the Philippines—seventeen at Del Monte and one that escaped destruction because it was on a reconnaissance flight—staged through Clark Field as long as it remained usable, picking up escorts from the battered fighter force and attacking the Japanese invaders. During one of these strikes, Capt. Colin P. Kelly, Jr., erroneously credited with sinking a battleship, remained at the controls of his burning B-17 until his crew had parachuted, sacrificing his life to save theirs and becoming one of the first American heroes of the air war.

The United States airmen in the Philippines, and those of the fledgling Philippine air arm, fought on as best they could, becoming infantrymen on the Bataan peninsula after their airplanes had been destroyed. The enemy overran Bataan in April 1942 and in May seized the island redoubt of Corregidor in Manila Bay. Organized resistance came to an end, but groups of Americans and Filipinos continued to wage guerrilla warfare against the Japanese.

During the course of the Philippines fighting, U.S. leadership changed. Brereton left Manila on Christmas Day of 1941 to participate in the unsuccessful defense of the Netherlands East Indies. His successor,

ABOVE: Capt. Colin P. Kelly, Jr., who as a lieutenant transferred from the Infantry to the Air Corps to learn to fly, remained at the controls of his burning B-17D so that his crew could parachute. LEFT: President Franklin D. Roosevelt called upon Congress to respond to Japan's "dastardly attack" on Pearl Harbor by declaring war.

A Chinese soldier stands guard over Curtiss P-40s bearing the tiger-shark nose design made popular by Claire L. Chennault's Flying Tigers, Americans who had volunteered to fight for China. Chennault's pilots, flying in two-aircraft teams, used the ruggedness, greater firepower, and armor protection of the P-40 against the more maneuverable Japanese planes, diving to make a single firing pass before breaking away.

Brig. Gen. Harold H. George, accompanied MacArthur when the latter departed in April 1942 to assume command in Australia.

Individual acts of heroism and stubborn, if ultimately unsuccessful, defensive fighting provided the only beacons of hope as Japan overran the far Pacific. At Wake Island, for instance, a Marine Corps fighter pilot, Capt. Henry T. Elrod, hit the Japanese destroyer *Kisaragi* with a pair of hundred-pound (45kg) bombs that set fires the crew could not extinguish. The ship exploded and sank with all hands. Elrod was killed by a sniper while fighting as an infantryman during the Japanese conquest of the island, which surrendered on December 23, 1941.

In Burma, the Flying Tigers, an outnumbered group of American mercenaries under contract to the Chinese

government, fought gallantly under the leadership of Claire L. Chennault, an officer retired from the Army Air Corps because of deafness. The Flying Tigers could not, however, prevent the Japanese from seizing Burma in May 1942 and closing the overland supply route to China. Until a new highway could be built, cargo destined for China would have to travel by air over the Himalayas.

By mid-March 1942, the enemy had also captured Hong Kong, all of Malaya as well as Singapore, and the Netherlands East Indies; shortly afterward, the Japanese sent warships into the Indian Ocean. In December 1941, during the invasion of Malaya, Japanese land-based torpedo planes had sunk HMS *Prince of Wales*, the battleship on which Roosevelt and Churchill had met at Placentia Bay, Newfoundland, earlier in the year, as well as the battle cruiser *Repulse*. In April 1942, Japanese carriers attacked Ceylon, sending two British cruisers and the carrier *Hermes* to the bottom of the Indian Ocean.

The Halsey-Doolittle Raid

As Adm. Nagumo, the victor at Pearl Harbor, withdrew from the Indian Ocean, the U.S. Navy was sending two of its precious aircraft carriers and their escort on a dangerous mission into Japanese waters. While USS *Enterprise* provided air cover, *Hornet* carried on its flight deck sixteen of the U.S. Army's North American B-25B medium bombers, commanded by Lt. Col. James H. Doolittle.

On April 18, a Japanese picket ship sighted the task force some 500 miles (800km) short of the planned launch point off Japan. The task force commander, Vice Adm. William F. Halsey, Jr., proposed launching the bombers immediately in case the Japanese vessel had sounded the alarm. Doolittle agreed, and as *Hornet* steamed into the wind, the bombers clawed their way aloft, the first time that any of the Army pilots had taken off from an aircraft carrier.

The bombers attacked targets in Tokyo, Kobe, and Nagoya, causing minor damage, before heading for the airfields in China where they were to land. Because of the longer flight, none of the planes had enough fuel to reach its destination. One crew landed at Vladivostok in the Soviet Union and was interned, but the others crash-landed or parachuted along the Chinese coastline. Of the seventy-nine airmen, three died in crash landings or when parachuting. Of the eight men the Japanese captured, one perished in prison, and three others were executed as war criminals.

British sailors abandon the doomed battleship *Prince of Wales* off the coast of Malaya after Japanese air attacks on December 10, 1941, and find refuge on a British destroyer. Aerial torpedoes also inflicted fatal damage on the battle cruiser *Repulse*.

A North American B-25B, its tail guns removed and a special sight installed for low-altitude bombing, thunders aloft from the deck of USS *Hornet* on April 18, 1942, for the first American air attack on Japan.

Code-Breaking, Coral Sea, and Midway

While Halsey and Doolittle raised American morale by bombing Japan, a group of cryptanalysts at Pearl Harbor under Lt. Comdr. Joseph J. Rochefort cracked the latest Japanese naval code, which employed printed books and tables rather than the machines used by Japanese diplomats or by the Germans. Rochefort's team warned that the Japanese were planning to seize Port Moresby, New Guinea, at a time when only two carriers, *Lexington* and *Yorktown*, could oppose them.

The enemy struck the first blow of the confused action known as the Battle of the Coral Sea on May 7, 1942, sinking an oiler, mistaken initially for an aircraft carrier, and a destroyer. Responding to a garbled sighting report of their own, United States aircraft found the Japanese carrier *Shoho* screening the Port Moresby invasion flotilla and sank the ship. On May 8, the main carrier forces located each other. American dive-bombers scored hits on *Shokaku*, but torpedo planes from *Zuikaku* inflicted fatal damage on *Lexington*, which had to be scuttled. Aircraft losses were roughly equal, but the Japanese sank a large carrier while losing a small one. Yet Japan's tactical victory became a strategic

ABOVE: Doolittle's raiders gather on the deck of USS *Hornet* in front of one of their B-25s. Standing in the left foreground are Lt. Col. James H. Doolittle (dark cap) and Capt. Marc Mitscher, the skipper of the *Hornet*.

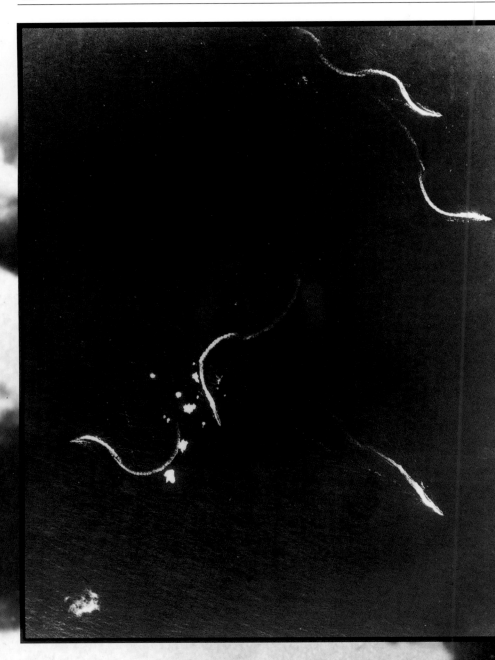

defeat; the attempt to seize Port Moresby and threaten Australia had to be abandoned, and *Shokaku* required repairs that kept it out of action for months.

Rochefort's code-breakers also discovered that the Japanese intended to push their perimeter eastward toward Hawaii by seizing Midway Island. Such an operation might lure the remnants of the Pacific Fleet into a decisive battle, and even if the U.S. Navy did not take the bait, possession of Midway would prevent repetition of the Halsey-Doolittle raid.

Adm. Yamamoto had produced an operations plan that required cooperation between Nagumo's carriers, the Midway invasion force, and the battle fleet and called for a diversionary attack in the Aleutians. Only the Aleutian operation went as planned. Carrier aircraft from *Junyo* and *Ryujo* bombed Dutch Harbor on June 3 and 4, and amphibious troops seized the islands of Attu and Kiska, although American forces recaptured Attu in May 1943, and in July the enemy abandoned Kiska.

A U.S. Navy PBY sighted the Midway-bound troop transports on June 3, and B-17s attacked but inflicted no damage. Nagumo's carriers, their position not yet known to the Americans, launched an attack on June 4 that brushed aside the fighters defending Midway, many of them obsolete Brewster F2A Buffaloes, and started spectacular fires on the island.

About 90 minutes after the first Zero fighter had taken off, another PBY reported the location of the Japanese carriers. The American carriers prepared to launch strikes, and the available aircraft on Midway delivered an attack of their own. Neither Air Forces B-17s and torpedo-carrying B-26s, nor Marine Corps dive-bombers, nor the Navy's new Grumman TBF torpedo planes succeeded in scoring any hits, but their determination, and reports from Japanese pilots over Midway, convinced Nagumo that another strike on the island would be necessary to capture the strategically located island.

ABOVE: The Brewster F2A Buffalo fighter was hopelessly outclassed by experienced Japanese fliers over Midway Island on June 4, 1942. An export version, however, enjoyed remarkable success in the hands of Finnish airmen against Soviet pilots.
LEFT: U.S. aerial torpedoes fatally damaged the Japanese carrier *Ryujo* in the Coral Sea on May 7, 1942.
OPPOSITE, INSET: Like insects skittering across the surface of a pond, Japanese ships in the Coral Sea maneuver to avoid aerial bombs in May 1942.

Nagumo, conscious perhaps of opportunities missed by not having launched a second attack on Pearl Harbor, decided to hit Midway again. He ordered the torpedoes and armor-piercing bombs removed from the aircraft standing by to attack the U.S. carriers and replaced with general-purpose munitions for attacking targets on the ground. At this point, a Japanese observation plane reported sighting the U.S. carrier task force. Faced with the job of rearming his aircraft with torpedoes and armor-piercing bombs, Nagumo demanded confirmation and was told a few minutes later that the U.S.ships were cruisers and destroyers, but he scarcely had relaxed when word came that the force included a carrier.

Once again, sailors replaced bomb loads on the hangar decks, but before the aircraft could take off, the returning Midway strike force had to land. Not until the proper bombs had been hung and the decks cleared

ABOVE: Smoke from burning oil-storage tanks blackens the skies over Midway Island after the Japanese air attack on June 4, 1942. The gooney birds in the foreground ignore the chaos. RIGHT: During the Battle of Midway, U.S. carrier aircraft crippled the cruiser *Mogami*, already damaged in a collision with another Japanese ship; *Mogami* survived to fall victim to an aerial attack at the Battle of Leyte Gulf in the autumn of 1944.

of returning aircraft could the rearmed planes take off to attack the three U.S. carriers, *Enterprise*, *Hornet*, and *Yorktown*. While these preparations went ahead, the Japanese had to maintain a combat air patrol to protect the ships, a task made all the more difficult by unreliable radar and communications, conditions affecting all the combatants at this stage of the war.

The American carriers launched their planes at extremely long range, hoping to catch the enemy as he refueled after bombing Midway, and the American aircraft tended to proceed in bunches rather than taking time to organize in balanced formations. Fighters thus became separated from the planes they were to escort. Some forty TBD torpedo planes found the Japanese carriers and bored in, even though they had no fighter cover. Although the slow, low-flying, and lightly armed torpedo bombers scored no hits, and only six of them returned, they attracted the Japanese fighters, clearing the way for U.S. dive-bombers to attack the fleet from higher altitudes.

In about six minutes, the SBDs sank or mortally damaged three aircraft carriers—*Kaga*, *Akagi*, and *Soryu*—all of which had attacked Pearl Harbor. A fourth Japanese carrier, *Hiryu*, escaped damage and launched a strike that crippled *Yorktown*, sunk on June 6 by a

Japanese submarine. By that time *Hiryu*, also a veteran of Pearl Harbor, had perished, fatally damaged on June 4 by dive-bombers from *Enterprise*.

Japan's shipbuilders would be hard-pressed to replace these carriers, but even more important, the Imperial Japanese Navy lost 322 aircraft and their veteran crews.

Midway blunted the cutting edge of Japan's naval aviation, and intense effort would be required to restore its sharpness. In short, Yamamoto's initial prediction seemed to be coming true; he ran wild for the first six months, but a Japanese victory was far from assured.

ABOVE: A Japanese torpedo plane dives past an escorting destroyer to attack the doomed aircraft carrier *Lexington* during the Battle of the Coral Sea. LEFT: Listing badly after an air attack on June 4, the aircraft carrier *Yorktown* lingered for two days until torpedoes from a Japanese submarine sealed its fate and sank a destroyer standing by.

Aerial Operations against the Germans, 1942

In Europe, the United States was building up its air power in the British Isles. The Eighth Air Force, under Maj. Gen. Carl Spaatz, became the principal Army Air Forces command there, and Brig. Gen. Ira Eaker's VIII Bomber Command would serve as Spaatz's striking force. The administrative and support elements of the Eighth Air Force began arriving in May 1942, some two months before the first B-17 touched down in Scotland.

The buildup, however, revealed flaws in aircrew training. Navigators and pilots had to sharpen their skills before trying to fly their bombers across the Atlantic by way of the new airfields in Greenland. When no bomber crew was available to navigate for a group of P-39s, the fighter unit left its aircraft behind, traveled by ship, and went into action flying borrowed Spitfires. Eaker also discovered that the bomber crews reaching the British Isles needed further training in formation flying and aerial gunnery, abilities absolutely essential for the daylight bombing of targets defended by fighters.

LEFT, TOP: The bombardier's position on the Handley Page Halifax. The camera lens distorts the view, emphasizing the isolation the bombardier must have felt in finding the target markers dropped by the pathfinders. LEFT, BOTTOM: The Handley Page Halifax VII descended from the bomber that, with the Stirling and Lancaster, battered German cities by night. Gone is the nose turret of the earlier version, which has been replaced by Plexiglas.

The crew of a Short Stirling poses on a bomb-loading cart. Handicapped by a lack of speed and a comparatively low operating ceiling, the Stirling proved vulnerable to both night fighters and antiaircraft fire. The Lancaster and Halifax replaced the Stirling in the bomber stream.

Senior British airmen remained patient while the VIII Bomber Command slowly gathered strength, even though those committed to "dehousing," like Air Marshal "Bomber" Harris, doubted that the Americans could accomplish much by daylight. In May 1941, the Royal Air Force had flown daytime test missions with twenty export versions of the B-17C, lost eight of the planes, and concluded that the Flying Fortress lacked adequate bomb capacity and defensive armament. Churchill's Secretary of State for Air, Sir Archibald Sinclair, nevertheless argued that the Americans deserved a chance to try their tactics. After all, if the VIII Bomber Command should succeed, the Allies would be able to bomb Germany night and day.

For now, however, Royal Air Force Bomber Command carried the war to Nazi-dominated Germany by night and by itself, using the four-engine Stirling, Halifax, and Lancaster. Harris's bombers burned the eastern German cities of Lübeck (where the Lancaster made its combat debut) and Rostock. On May 30, 1942, a thousand planes battered Cologne, though some were shifted for the night from crew-training duties.

Not until June 10 did American bombers join in, and when they did, they flew from North Africa, not from England, against Romania rather than Germany, bombing at dawn rather than during the day. A detachment of B-24s en route to China was held in Egypt because Japanese troops reacted to Doolittle's bombing raid by seizing the air bases from which his B-25s and the heavier B-24s would have operated. A dozen of the B-24 Liberators flew by night to Ploesti in Romania and at daybreak bombed the refineries there, inflicting no damage but losing no aircraft to enemy action.

In a symbolic gesture, six Eighth Air Force crews, flying A-20 light bombers borrowed from the Royal Air Force, joined an equal number of British aircraft of the same type and on July 4, 1942, attacked German airfields in Holland. Only two of the bombers flown by Americans succeeded in finding and attacking the assigned target. The Eighth Air Force lost two planes, and the British lost one.

Eaker's B-17s went to war on August 17, when he personally took part in a twelve-plane daylight strike against the Sotteville railroad yard at Rouen, France.

Four squadrons of Spitfires escorted the formation, which bombed accurately and suffered superficial damage to just one B-17. Although the attack at Sotteville did not affect the course of the war, the token raid signaled that the VIII Bomber Command intended to become a full partner in the bomber offensive to come.

El Alamein and Stalingrad: The Limits of Hitler's Conquests

While the Americans slowly gathered strength for an Anglo-American bomber offensive, German troops advancing on the Suez Canal succumbed to fatigue, shortages of supplies, and strong defenses, as their offensive ground to a halt in July 1942 at El Alamein in the Egyptian desert.

A series of attacks and counterattacks ensued, but not until October and November could the British and Commonwealth forces crack the German line and begin pursuing the enemy westward. During the breakthrough

The tail section of a downed He 111 litters a street in Stalingrad in the summer of 1942; a burned-out building looms in the background.

Because the desert restricted motor convoys to the coastline where roads and ports were few, air power could readily interfere with the movement of Axis supplies and reinforcements. A Bristol Blenheim is being loaded with light bombs for a 1940 attack on the Italian base at Bardia, Libya.

The Luftwaffe and the Battle for Kharkov

Both Hitler and Stalin took a personal hand in setting the stage for the battle at Kharkov in the Ukraine. Stalin insisted that his generals counterattack the advancing Germans at every opportunity, and Hitler looked to the Luftwaffe to provide an aerial fire brigade to help extinguish Soviet resistance.

At Kharkov, a Soviet counterattack, spearheaded by tanks and supported by fighters and ground-support planes, overran German positions on May 14, 1942, threatening to isolate the city. Some of the Soviet fighters were new models, comparable to Hitler's Messerschmitts, but others were obsolete I-15s and I-16s, types that had fought in Spain. The deadliest Soviet plane, however, proved to be the Ilyushin Il-2 Stormovik, a single-engine attack craft with armor that enabled it to survive small-arms and even light anti-aircraft fire as it engaged German tanks and troops with two 20mm cannon, two light machine guns, rockets, and bombs.

To meet the threat, Hitler turned to his fire brigade, and the Luftwaffe shifted air-craft from as far away as the Crimea and the approaches to Moscow. The added aerial firepower helped restore a defensive line within three days. The newly arrived aircraft included the latest Me 109s (the G model), Ju 87D dive-bombers, Heinkel 111 bombers, and twin-engine Junkers Ju 88s, which doubled as dive-bombers and horizontal bombers. The Me 109s drove Soviet fighters from the sky, and the bombers and dive-bombers took a hand in the confused fighting.

Since German troops could not make direct radio contact with the supporting air-craft, they had to rely on Luftwaffe liaison officers to forward to higher headquarters all requests for air strikes and on identification panels, flares, and smoke pots to mark front-line positions. Amid the smoke and dust of battle, signals proved hard to see from the air, and in some cases troops under fire could not set out their identification panels. As a result, German bombs sometimes fell on friendly units.

Despite the occasional accident, tactical aviation helped the Germans encircle the Soviet troops who had counterattacked at Kharkov, killing as many as 75,000 and capturing some 239,000. The most heavily engaged flying unit, Fliegerkorps IV (the Fourth Air Corps), flew more than 15,000 sorties, dropping almost 8,000 tons (7,200t) of bombs, some 8 million surrender leaflets, and more than 380 canisters of supplies for isolated units. Trimotor Junkers Ju 52 transports delivered 1,545 tons (1,390t) of cargo to air-fields used by the Fourth Air Corps. The command lost 49 aircraft and 110 airmen killed or missing, but it claimed the destruction of 615 Soviet aircraft, more than 200 tanks, some 3,000 trucks, and more than 1,600 horse-drawn vehicles.

Although more fully mechanized—and possessing better aerial resupply—than during the Polish campaign and the conquest of western Europe, German soldiers sometimes had to rely on their own muscles to move equipment during the invasion of the Soviet Union in 1941.

and pursuit, the independent Royal Air Force collabo-
rated with the ground forces; the army commander,
Gen. Bernard Law Montgomery, and the air commander,
Air Vice Marshal Sir Arthur Coningham, maintained a
joint headquarters and cooperated as equals.

While Hitler's designs on the Suez Canal were
being frustrated, his forces in the Soviet Union began
encountering reverses after winning a succession of victories, as at Kharkov in the spring of 1942. A German
attack launched in August 1942 against Stalingrad on the
Volga River bogged down after a three-month struggle to
capture the ruined city. Soviet forces counterattacked in
November and surrounded the Germans. Attempts to
break through to the trapped army or supply it by air
failed, and the starving survivors gave up in January
1943. The battle of Stalingrad resulted in the death or
capture of some 200,000 German soldiers.

At Stalingrad and El Alamein, Nazi Germany
reached the limits of its conquests.

Before the tide of battle turned
against them, these German
soldiers posed at Stalingrad
with a light machine gun.

Chapter 5

Conquering Northwest Africa and Italy

ON NOVEMBER 8, 1942, ANGLO-AMERICAN FORCES INVADED THE FRENCH colonies of northwest Africa, in part to divert German pressure from the Soviet Union. The invasion, Operation Torch, afforded an opportunity to trap Field Marshal Erwin Rommel's Afrika Korps, retreating westward from El Alamein.

The French garrison at Algiers, Algeria, offered only light resistance, but the defenders of Casablanca, Morocco, and Oran, Algeria, proved stubborn. Even so, the Allies captured all three objectives by November 11, enabling the eastward deployment to begin. When Maj. Gen. Dwight D. Eisenhower's Torch force advanced, it moved as two national contingents, each with its own command structure and air support.

The Advance into Tunisia

On the day after the Torch landings, German troops began arriving in Tunisia, initially by air, with as many as fifty Junkers trimotors landing at Tunis in a single day. Luftwaffe fighters and bombers also deployed to Tunisia.

LEFT: Italian-based Consolidated B-24 Liberators of the Fifteenth Air Force, now fitted with a power-operated nose turret, brave intense German antiaircraft fire on May 31, 1944, during a high-altitude attack on oil refineries at Ploesti, Romania.

The weather slowed the Allied advance, however. Rain turned roads and forward airfields to mud, and the Allies, short of aircraft, lacked long-range fighters to operate from all-weather airfields to the rear and tangle with the Luftwaffe units, operating from hard-surfaced airfields unaffected by winter rains in Tunisia.

To speed the movement of the Twelfth Air Force—commanded by Jimmy Doolittle, now a major general—Eisenhower summoned General Spaatz from the Eighth Air Force in England to serve as acting Deputy Chief of Staff for Air. Spaatz helped redistribute aerial resources between the British and Americans and obtained engineers to build advance airstrips. On January 5, 1943, he assumed command of Allied Air Forces in North Africa, overseeing both Doolittle and his British counterpart, Air Marshal Sir William Welsh.

At the time of Torch, U.S. Army tactical air doctrine called for the commander of the Air Support Command of a theater air force to advise the commander of the principal ground unit on the employment of aviation. In northwest Africa, Brig. Gen. Howard A. Craig, commanding the air support component of Doolittle's Twelfth Air Force, dealt with the American corps commander, Lt. Gen. Lloyd R. Fredendall. The corps commander nominated targets, and the airman decided how to attack them.

ABOVE: The Douglas C-47, a military version of the DC-3 commercial transport, proved a workhorse throughout the war, delivering cargo and passengers, towing gliders, and dropping paratroops and their supplies. LEFT: The twin-engine Junkers Ju 88 succeeded as a dive-bomber, horizontal bomber, and night fighter. Some night fighter versions carried cannon mounted behind the cockpit to fire generally upward, enabling the pilot to silhouette a bomber against the sky—or spot its engine exhaust—and open fire from below.

ABOVE: Field Marshal Erwin Rommel, the Desert Fox, left Tunisia to assume a command in western Europe. Wounded by a strafing British fighter, he was convalescing when implicated in the plot to kill Hitler. Because of his popularity with the German people, Rommel was allowed to commit suicide instead of being tried and executed.
RIGHT: President Franklin D. Roosevelt and Prime Minister Winston Churchill met with their principal advisers at Casablanca in January 1943. Two French representatives also attended — Gen. Henri Giraud (on the far left) and Gen. Charles de Gaulle (second from right).

The British system of equality between air and ground commanders, which reflected the independence of the Royal Air Force, was of great interest to the leaders of the Army Air Forces, even though General Arnold had tacitly agreed to postpone the campaign for achieving parity with the Army until the war was over. In return, Marshall had pledged to give the air arm as much autonomy within the Army as Arnold believed was necessary.

Moreover, the team of Montgomery and Coningham had harried the Afrika Korps throughout its retreat to Tunisia, whereas the American team of Doolittle, Craig, and Fredendall moved more slowly. At first glance, different command arrangements seemed responsible, but that interpretation ignored the fact that Montgomery and Coningham had been pursuing and attacking, in good weather, an enemy low on fuel and supplies and confined to a narrow coastal track.

In contrast, Fredendall was slogging through mud to forestall a German buildup, while both Craig and Doolittle suffered from tenuous supply lines and a shortage of aircraft. Despite these problems, Craig and his successor, Col. Paul Williams, reported excellent relations with Fredendall, who tended to give them free rein. Weather, experience, and number of aircraft—rather than parity between air and ground—gave the British commanders the edge.

Circumstances, as well as undeniable skill, made Coningham the man of the hour. During an overhaul of command arrangements in the Mediterranean—one of the initiatives that, like the invasion of Sicily and the Combined Bomber Offensive, stemmed from the January 1943 Casablanca Conference, attended by Roosevelt and Churchill—Eisenhower chose Coningham to head the Northwest Africa Tactical Air Force. Coningham's organization formed one component of

the Northwest Africa Air Forces, under Spaatz; another element was Doolittle's strategic air force.

Until the point that Coningham arrived in Tunisia, Brig. Gen. Laurence S. Kuter, an American, commanded tactical aviation. On February 19, 1943, during this transition, Rommel, who had taken over the German forces in Tunisia, took advantage of weather that grounded Allied fighters and counterattacked at Kasserine Pass, driving back Fredendall's troops. Rommel lacked the manpower to consolidate his gains, but his sudden thrust caused Eisenhower to replace Fredendall with Lt. Gen. George S. Patton, Jr.

Patton Clashes with Coningham

Coningham found the abrasive Patton more difficult than even the egotistic Montgomery. The American general became convinced that his troops were not receiving adequate support from Coningham and angrily complained in his daily situation report for April 1 that "total lack of air cover for our units has allowed the German Air Force to operate at will." The usually affable Coningham retaliated by charging that Patton's soldiers were not "battleworthy." To prevent the quarrel from disrupting the war in Tunisia, Air Chief Marshal Sir Arthur Tedder, Coningham's superior, ordered him to apologize, and he obeyed, describing the incident as a misunderstanding.

Patton, however, insisted on complaining to Spaatz and Tedder. As they conferred, four German fighters strafed the site of the meeting, demonstrating that Coningham did not rule the skies. A delighted Patton declared that if he could find the names of the Luftwaffe pilots, he would "mail each one of them a medal."

The quarrel between Patton and Coningham did not delay the conquest of Tunisia. Ultra intelligence reported the schedules of aerial and sea convoys carrying troops from Sicily, bringing about the Palm Sunday massacre of April 18, 1943, when Allied fighters shot down fifty to seventy transports—Junkers trimotors and six-engine Messerschmitt Me 323s—and sixteen escorting fighters. Rommel left to help defend France against a cross-channel attack, and his successor, Gen. Jurgen von Arnim, surrendered on May 12, 1943.

Coequal and Interdependent

The collaboration in North Africa between Montgomery and Coningham inspired a new War Department Field Manual, FM 100-20, which declared that "land power and air power" were "coequal and interdependent" and that "neither was an auxiliary of the other."

The manual declared that an "air force commander" should exercise centralized control over aviation and avoid attaching air units to ground commanders. Gen. Marshall, as Army Chief of Staff, approved the manual without submitting it to review by the War Department General Staff. He thus indicated his likely support for an independent postwar air force and, perhaps, strengthened the authority of Eaker, the senior American airman in the United Kingdom, to conduct the strategic bombing that would defeat Germany and ensure independence.

Ironically, the spirit of cooperation between Montgomery and Coningham vanished during the battle for France. The ground commander insisted that Coningham bomb French villages to create roadblocks, but the airman refused, realizing that civilians would die in attacks that would barely inconvenience the Germans. Montgomery tried unsuccessfully to have Coningham replaced, but the crisis passed.

ABOVE: Two masters of tactical aviation: Air Vice Marshal Sir Arthur Coningham (RIGHT) teamed with Marshal Bernard Law Montgomery in North Africa and assumed command of the 2d Allied Tactical Air Force for the invasion of Europe.

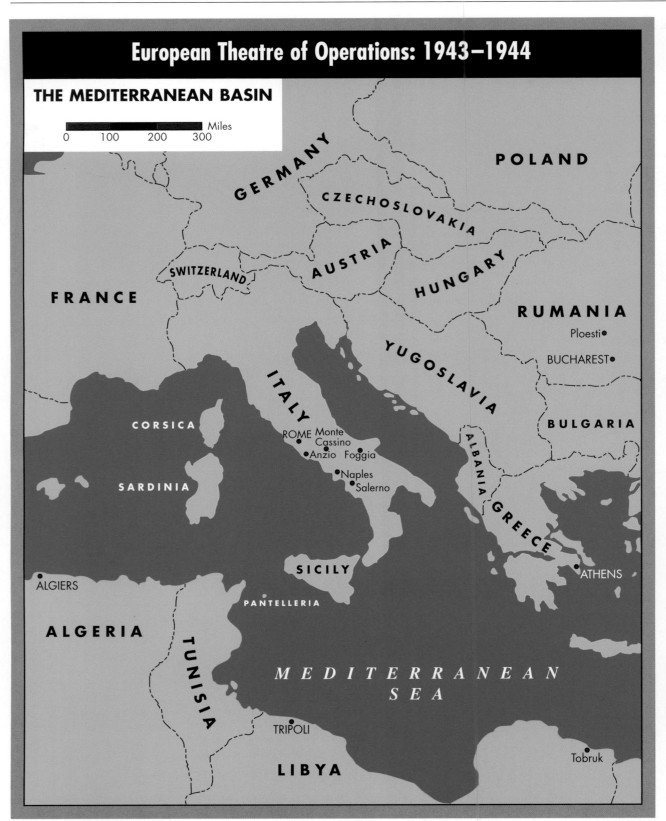

European Theatre of Operations: 1943–1944

THE MEDITERRANEAN BASIN

Miles
0   100   200   300

GERMANY

POLAND

CZECHOSLOVAKIA

SWITZERLAND

AUSTRIA

HUNGARY

FRANCE

RUMANIA

Ploesti

BUCHAREST

YUGOSLAVIA

ITALY

CORSICA

ROME
Monte Cassino
Anzio   Foggia

BULGARIA

ALBANIA

SARDINIA

Naples
Salerno

GREECE

SICILY

ATHENS

ALGIERS

PANTELLERIA

ALGERIA

TUNISIA

MEDITERRANEAN SEA

TRIPOLI

Tobruk

LIBYA

Northwest Africa seemed to offer a means of easing pressure on the Soviet Union and trapping the Axis forces retreating westward from El Alamein, Egypt. The Germans rushed reinforcements into Tunisia and prolonged the fighting there until May 1943.

The Allies, rather than allow the victorious forces in North Africa to lose their fighting edge, invaded Sicily and then Italy, becoming drawn into a campaign of attrition that tied down both Allied and Axis troops. An invasion of southern France in August 1945 enabled the western Allies to form a front against Germany that stretched from the North Sea to Switzerland, while Soviet forces continued their advance from the east.

The fighting in North Africa taught Allied airmen valuable lessons of air-ground cooperation applied during subsequent operations on the European continent. Sicily saw the introduction of airborne troops, though with less success than in Normandy. Italy provided bases for strategic bombing in southern Germany and eastern Europe, but aerial interdiction achieved more impressive results in the Rhône Valley of France than in Italy.

Gen. Dwight D. Eisenhower (center), the Supreme Allied Commander in Europe, visits an airfield where a British medium bomber unit is based. Behind Eisenhower is Air Vice Marshal Sir Arthur Coningham, commander of the 2d Tactical Air Force. The others (clockwise from Coningham) are Air Chief Marshal Sir Trafford Leigh-Mallory, later killed in a crash; Maj. Gen. Hoyt S. Vandenberg, who would become Chief of Staff of the independent Air Force; Group Capt. C.R. Dunlap, commander of the medium bomber outfit; and Lt. Gen. Lewis H. Brereton, in command of the Ninth Air Force.

The Tuskegee Airmen

Over Pantelleria, African-American pilots, trained at the Tuskegee Army Airfield in Alabama, entered combat for the first time.

In 1940 Congress had admitted blacks to a civilian pilot training program designed to create a reservoir of trained fliers that the armed forces might tap in case of war, but the Army rejected every black who applied for the Air Corps. Those turned down included Benjamin O. Davis, Jr., who graduated from the Military Academy in 1936, the first African American to do so since 1889. General Arnold explained that the racially segregated Air Corps had no black aviation units in which an African American could serve.

Pressure from black leaders and their allies in the Roosevelt administration and Congress forced the Army to launch the training program at Tuskegee, which produced the racially segregated fighter squadron that fought at Pantelleria—expanded to a four-squadron group that served in Europe—and a bombardment group that did not go overseas. After training at Tuskegee, Davis commanded the initial squadron and, later, a group.

Graduates of the pilot training program at Tuskegee Army Airfield in Alabama receive last-minute instructions before taking off from their Italian base on a fighter mission. After their combat debut over Pantelleria, members of the first class of African-American air cadets fought in Italy, where they sank a German destroyer and escorted bombers based at Foggia against targets in Europe.

Crossing the Mediterranean

The Casablanca Conference, besides placing Coningham in charge of the Northwest Africa Tactical Air Force, also approved the invasion of Sicily, but before attacking, the Allies had to capture Pantelleria, a volcanic island that could have served the Axis as a staging area and therefore seemed too dangerous to ignore.

For ten days, warships pounded the island and bombers dropped some 4,800 tons (4,320t) of explosives. Then on June 11, 1943, as the assault force started toward shore, the Italian defenders surrendered, both morale and defenses shattered.

Allied airborne troops made three nighttime landings in Sicily. The first, on the night of July 9, hours before the next morning's amphibious assault, encountered high winds that scattered the U.S. parachutists and British gliders. Only a dozen of 133 gliders landed as planned, and 65 came down at sea.

Two nights later, 144 C-47s carrying U.S. paratroops came under both friendly and German fire, losing 23 transports. Allied ships had not received notice of the night's mission, and the Germans had reoccupied the drop zone. Coordination again failed on July 13, when British paratroops also came under friendly fire, losing 11 of 124 aircraft. In every case, however, the airborne unit managed to consolidate and attain its objective, at least partially.

Despite the airborne misadventures, Allied forces pushed on. The imminent loss of Sicily toppled Mussolini from power on July 25, 1943. The Sicilian campaign ended on August 17 when Allied troops entered Messina, too late to prevent an orderly withdrawal to the Italian peninsula.

The Raid on Ploesti

During the fight for Sicily, Maj. Gen. Brereton, who had taken over command of the Ninth Air Force in North Africa, drilled two of his B-24 groups and three borrowed from the Eighth Air Force to raid the oil refineries at Ploesti, Romania.

On August 1, 177 B-24s took off from Libyan airfields for a rooftop attack rather than the high-altitude

PAGE 77: A Consolidated B-24D skims over the burning Astra Romana oil refinery at Ploesti, Romania. Despite this attack, which ignited spectacular fires on August 1, 1943, and subsequent raids, Ploesti continued to produce at least a trickle of fuel until overrun by Soviet troops in August 1944.

RIGHT: North American B-25s fly over the Volturno River in November 1943 after bombing German positions in Italy. The B-25 bombed Japan in April 1942 and saw extensive service with the Army Air Forces in the Pacific as well as in North Africa and Europe. As the PBJ patrol bomber, the plane also flew for the Navy and Marine Corps.

precision bombing for which the Liberator had been designed. Off the coast of Greece, the bomber carrying the navigator for the formation suddenly dived into the sea, for no known reason. The B-24 carrying the back-up navigator dropped down to search fruitlessly for survivors, could not catch up with the formation, and returned to North Africa. Less experienced officers had to navigate. German radar picked up the B-24s and tracked them until they dropped too low for coverage. Warned of the impending raid, antiaircraft gunners readied their weapons, and fifty-two German and Romanian fighters took off to intercept.

Without the lead navigator and his designated replacement, two of the bombardment groups missed a checkpoint, heading in the wrong direction and throwing the plan of attack into confusion. Some crews found

their targets already ablaze and had to fly through flame and blinding smoke, risking explosions from delayed-action bombs.

The airmen pressed the attack; Second Lieutenant Lloyd D. Hughes, for example, bored through a fiery curtain that ignited fuel gushing from damaged tanks. He kept his burning Liberator in the air long enough to drop its bombs, but only two gunners survived a crash landing. Hughes (posthumously) was one of five officers awarded the Medal of Honor for heroism during the Ploesti raid.

Despite spectacular explosions and fires, the bombing did not cause a protracted drop in fuel production, in part because previously idle facilities took up the slack. Antiaircraft fire, fighters, and accidents destroyed fifty-four U.S. bombers; more than 500 crewmen were killed or captured. The losses, however, did not prevent the Ninth Air Force from dispatching sixty-five B-24s to attack an aircraft factory at Wiener-Neustadt in German-annexed Austria on August 13.

Invading Italy

After the conquest of Sicily, the Allies focused on main-land Italy, where King Victor Emmanuel had secretly agreed to surrender even before British troops landed on September 3, 1943, at the heel and toe of the boot-shaped peninsula. Plans called for a daring airborne raid on Rome to rescue the king, but the operation had to be canceled after a last-minute reconnaissance revealed that the Germans were too strong. The king got away never-theless, and on September 8 Italy announced its surren-der to the Allies.

On September 9, the day after Italy's surrender, the Allies landed at Salerno in an attempt to seize the port

ABOVE: A posturing Benito Mussolini shares the front row of a reviewing stand with Adolf Hitler and the king and queen of Italy. Mussolini fell from power after the Axis defeat in Sicily, King Victor Emmanuel defected to the Allies in September 1943, and in October Italy declared war on Germany. LEFT: An Allied ship loaded with ammunition explodes during the invasion of Sicily.

An American tank rolls off a landing craft to move ashore on Sicily.

of Naples. The Luftwaffe fought back, punching holes in the air cover provided by aircraft from five British escort carriers and the recently captured airfields in Sicily. German planes attacked the beachhead, and radio-guided bombs damaged three Allied warships. Air Forces C-47s parachuted reinforcements that helped hold the Salerno beaches until the Germans on the heights above began withdrawing. On October 1, the Americans entered Naples, and the British advancing from the south overran the airfields at Foggia, within bomber range of southern Germany and eastern Europe. Twelve days after the capture of Naples, Italy declared war on Germany.

The Italian campaign, which began as an attempt to make productive use of troops that would have been idle after the victories in North Africa and Sicily, was becoming a strategic dead end, tying down Allied as well as German forces with no prospect of decisive results. To break the developing stalemate, the Allies on January 22, 1944, landed at Anzio in an amphibious end run designed to capture Rome. The landing force failed to break through, however, held in check by German troops deployed from as far away as Yugoslavia.

Troops advancing toward Anzio from the south collided with determined German resistance at Monte Cassino, the site of a Benedictine monastery which traced its origins to the sixth century. Eaker, recently transferred to the Mediterranean theater when Arnold

grew impatient with the progress of the air war against Germany, became convinced that German observers were directing artillery fire from the mountaintop abbey. The enemy actually had no soldiers within the monastery, though some did man positions 50 yards (45m) outside the walls, but Eaker did what he thought necessary.

On February 15, after scattering leaflets warning the monks to flee, Allied airmen dropped some 600 tons (540t) of bombs on the mountaintop, while artillery added to the destruction. After the bombardment, Germans dug in among the ruins, and some four months passed before the capture of Monte Cassino and a link-up with the Anzio beachhead.

Operation Strangle

Eaker now sold Arnold on Operation Strangle, a plan to "reduce the enemy's flow of supplies to a level which will make it impractical to maintain and operate his forces in Central Italy." Eaker believed Strangle would end the stalemate in Italy through air power and prevent ground commanders from reversing the results of the North African campaign, regaining control of tactical aviation, and routinely diverting strategic bombers to tactical missions.

During Operation Strangle, Allied aircraft attacked rail yards, railroad and highway bridges, and road and rail traffic. The Allies, however, could not bomb accurately by night. Consequently, trains and trucks rolled through the darkness; work went ahead after dark on damaged roads, rail lines, and bridges; and vehicles shuttled cargo past construction sites. The Germans kept sufficient cargo moving south to prevent a collapse as they grudgingly gave ground, but they could not ship enough supplies for a counteroffensive.

The German retreat, moreover, shortened supply lines and made them less vulnerable to aerial attack, and pressure on the Germans declined after the capture of Rome, on June 5, 1944, for on the following day, the Allies invaded Normandy, making Italy a secondary theater of war.

Not until May 2, 1945, did the Germans in Italy finally surrender.

A Boeing B-17 drops a string of bombs through cloud cover during the Italian campaign. The chin, dorsal, belly, and tail turrets are clearly visible as are the port-side waist gunner's position and the manually operated machine gun poking upward from the radio operator's position aft of the cockpit.

Chapter 6

The Defeat of Germany

BESIDES APPROVING THE SICILIAN AND ITALIAN CAMPAIGNS, THE CASABLANCA Conference of January 1943 paved the way for the Anglo-American Combined Bomber Offensive. When Churchill summoned Eaker to Casablanca, the latter had not yet gone to the Mediterranean and launched Operation Strangle. The general still commanded the Britain-based U.S. bombers and was determined to gain the prime minister's support for daylight attacks on German industry instead of such targets as submarine pens.

Churchill, however, wanted an explanation as to why Eaker had yet to drop his first bomb on Germany. Rather than explain past failure, the American described a successful future in which he would pound Germany by day while Air Marshal Harris kept hammering away by night. Churchill put aside his doubts about daytime attacks and vowed "to bomb the devils round-the-clock," as Eaker had proposed.

Eaker had achieved his primary purpose, getting a chance to conduct daylight bombing. His second goal was to make sure that VIII Bomber Command did not become the mere instrument of Harris and his veteran Bomber Command. With the backing of Marshall, the Army Chief of Staff, Eaker again succeeded; the Royal Air Force would honor the prewar understanding that gave Americans autonomy from the United Kingdom in tactics and targeting during operations.

The Anglo-American Combined Chiefs of Staff—the military, naval, and air leadership of both nations—established a general objective for the bombing campaign, allowing Eaker and Harris

LEFT: As the air war against Hitler increases in fury, a B-17 passes over the day's target which is already obscured by exploding bombs.

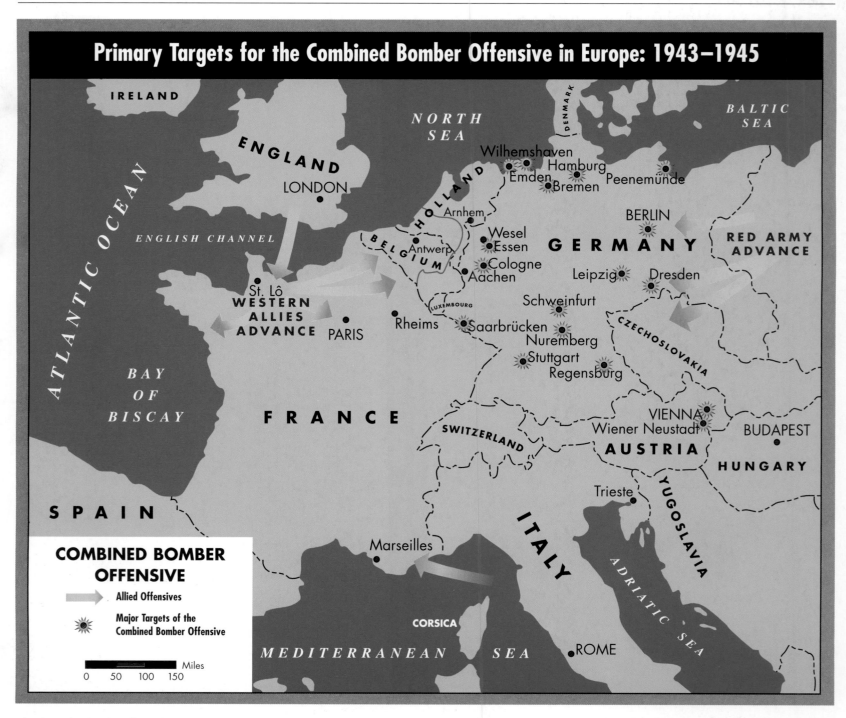

Primary Targets for the Combined Bomber Offensive in Europe: 1943–1945

COMBINED BOMBER OFFENSIVE

→ Allied Offensives

✷ Major Targets of the Combined Bomber Offensive

Miles
0   50   100   150

When the Combined Bomber Offensive began in 1943, air power provided the only readily available means of damaging Hitler's war machine and easing pressure on the Soviet Union. Peripheral amphibious and ground operations in North Africa, Sicily, and Italy caused attrition, but only aerial bombardment seemed capable of destroying factories and refineries, demoralizing the labor force, and cutting off the fuel and equipment necessary for modern warfare.

Once it clamped its jaws on oil production, the Combined Bomber Offensive threatened the survival of the German war machine, but the systematic attack on the fuel industry did not gather momentum until after the Western Allies had stormed ashore in France. Soviet forces advancing inexorably from the east and the other Allies attacking from Normandy and the Riviera forced an increasingly desperate enemy to expend oil, men, and machines in a futile struggle. Hitler's dream of a falling out between the United States and the Soviet Union did not materialize until long after troops from the two nations had met on the Elbe River and Germany lay in ruins.

to pursue the goal as they wished. After the Casablanca Conference, the Combined Chiefs of Staff called for the "progressive destruction and dislocation of the German military, industrial, and economic system, and the undermining of the morale of the German people to a point where their capacity for armed resistance is fatally weakened."

This statement of policy ultimately evolved into the Pointblank Directive, which was approved by the

Combined Chiefs in May 1943, and made the bomber offensive a "prerequisite" to the invasion of France. In carrying out the directive, Harris proposed to continue blasting cities by night, while Eaker emphasized the importance of gaining control of the daylight skies by bombing the aircraft industry and in the process shooting down German fighters.

General Eaker's VIII Bomber Command had wasted much of the autumn before the Casablanca sessions

Protected by steel-reinforced concrete, U-boat pens, like this one at Cherbourg on the French coast, proved impervious to the heaviest bombs the B-17 and B-24 could carry.

By the end of the war, repeated Allied bombing had destroyed the port facilities at Wilhelmshaven, which in January 1943 had been the first target in Germany attacked by American bombers.

attacking submarine shelters along the French coast, a futile undertaking since the heaviest bomb carried by the B-17 or B-24 could not penetrate the steel-reinforced concrete shielding the U-boats. Air power would help defeat German submarines not through these attacks but with raids on U-boat construction yards, patrol bombers ranging out to sea, blimps keeping watch over coastal shipping, and ultimately, escort carriers accompanying convoys across the Atlantic.

During the weeks following the Casablanca Conference, Eaker's bombers at last carried the war to

Germany. On January 27, a force of fifty-five B-17s started off to hit Vegesack, but they were thwarted when they encountered thick clouds; fifty-three of them instead bombed Wilhelmshaven, a secondary target.

The Battle of the Ruhr

While the American B-17s and B-24s tested the daylight defenses of Germany, Air Marshal Harris fought the Battle of the Ruhr.

Between July and March 1943, pathfinders—flying the de Havilland Mosquito, a fast, twin-engine, plywood aircraft—benefitted from navigation beams precise enough to pinpoint a specific building while marking targets in the region's industrial cities. Essen and other cities underwent nighttime pummeling, and on May 16, 1943, a specially trained group of Lancasters, led by Wing Comdr. Guy Gibson, tried to cut off hydroelectric power to the Ruhr. The bombers swept low over the waters impounded by the Mohne and Eder dams and breached those structures with bombs designed expressly for the purpose, but failed to silence the factories of the Ruhr.

In attacking targets such as Essen, Bomber Command encountered the defense system prepared by Gen. Josef Kammhuber, who had created a double row of defensive boxes along the perimeter of Nazi-occupied Europe, backed by other boxes clustered around Berlin. Within each box, a long-range Freya, an early warning

radar, detected the bombers, tracked them, and handed on responsibility for their interception to a pair of shorter-range but more precise Wurzburg radars that were able to sharply define a target within a range of 30 miles (48km).

One Wurzburg tracked an approaching bomber—one element in an unevenly spaced stream of aircraft rather than part of a precise formation—while the other tracked a night fighter. A controller coached the fighter into position to see and attack the bomber. Some of the twin-engine night fighters—the best were modified Ju 88s and Me 110s—mounted a short-range but fairly precise Lichtenstein radar, and single-engine day fighters, such as the Focke Wulf Fw 190, might also harry the bombers, their pilots sometimes spotting bombers in searchlight beams or silhouetted against a burning city. Kammhuber's system favored tight control from the ground rather than individual initiative by the airborne interceptors.

ABOVE: Ira Eaker, shown as a brigadier general, in August 1942 led the first strike by U.S. strategic bombers against a target in Nazi-occupied Europe; in June 1944, he led the first shuttle-bombing mission between Italy and the Soviet Union. LEFT: The Focke Wulf Fw 190 outperformed its predecessor, the Me 109, functioning as a daylight interceptor, a fighter-bomber, and a Wild Boar night fighter, freelancing without precise radar control.

A crew member of a Boeing B-17 shoves packets of Window through a slot in the radio compartment of a B-17. When the Americans first began using Window, some of the men dispensing the foil had not been told to separate the packets and instead pushed unopened bundles out of a hatch.

Window Attacks German Radar

By the summer of 1943, Bomber Command stood ready to assault the key element in Kammhuber's system— radar. The weapon, code-named Window, consisted of strips of aluminum foil, bundled by the thousands and released by the millions. As the strips fluttered to earth, they reflected radar waves, creating echoes that in effect blinded the system and concealed the bombers.

The British delayed using Window to avoid revealing it to the enemy, but the technique was not unique to them. Japanese airmen had already used a similar device, though on a small scale, and the Germans had developed a version of their own, tested it, and become so concerned by its effectiveness that they refused to use it, lest the British copy the discovery.

As the Germans had feared, Window paralyzed Kammhuber's defenses on the night of July 24–25, 1943, when Bomber Command made the first in a series of four raids against Hamburg. During the second night of bombing, July 27–28, the defenders made greater use of freelancing day fighters, nicknamed Wild Boars, which had no radar. The Tame Boars, radar-equipped night fighters, discovered that they had better luck with Lichtenstein at high altitude, where the bundles of foil had just opened and the radar-blinding curtain of Window had not yet formed. Controllers on the ground found that Wurzburg was more vulnerable than Freya to the effects of Window; they began concentrating on tracking the bomber stream and reporting its course to the fighters, since precise interceptions were no longer possible.

Despite these early attempts to cope with Window, the second raid hit the city and set it ablaze, creating a firestorm with temperatures of 1500 degrees Fahrenheit (800°C) that sucked oxygen at hurricane force from the surrounding neighborhoods and consumed an area of four square miles (10.4 square km).

Harris's airmen bombed Hamburg again on the nights of July 29–30 and August 2–3, with mixed results. Civilian casualties in the four raids totaled some 45,000, perhaps 40,000 of them victims of the firestorm. Bomber Command lost eighty-seven aircraft, fifty-nine of them shot down by fighters, and twice that number were damaged.

During the series of night raids, the VIII Bomber Command struck Hamburg twice by day, bombing the shipyards on July 25 and July 26 but inflicting minor damage. A total of 146 B-17s, out of 252 dispatched, dropped 306 tons (275t) of bombs, losing 17 Flying Fortresses, roughly twice the loss rate experienced by the British. Smoke from fires set by the first British raid obscured aiming points, especially on July 25, and may have caused some bombers to search for alternate targets.

Schweinfurt and Regensburg

On August 17, 1943, Eaker launched his most ambitious operation of the war thus far, sending one mission against the ball-bearing factories at Schweinfurt while another was bombing an aircraft plant at Regensburg and continuing to airfields in North Africa.

Since the newly arrived Republic P-47B Thunderbolt—a barrel-shaped, single-engine fighter mounting eight .50-caliber machine guns—accommodated only a small external fuel tank, it could escort the bombers no farther than Aachen. As a result, the bombers would have to rely on their own machine guns against German fighters. The better to mass their firepower, the bomber crews trained to fly in a cumbersome fifty-four-plane combat wing consisting of three eighteen-plane groups staggered over a width of 7,000 feet (2,135m), a height of 1,000 feet (305m), and a depth of 1,800 feet (550m).

The 146 B-17s of the Regensburg force were to take off first, fight their way to the target, and continue to North Africa. The Schweinfurt mission would follow a short time later, entering Germany as the interceptors that had opposed the other formation were landing for

fuel and ammunition, and afterward returning to the United Kingdom. Unfortunately, the uneven training of Eaker's airmen disrupted the timing. The Regensburg mission, under Brig. Gen Curtis E. LeMay, climbed through thick fog, organized into combat wings, and headed for the target, but the Schweinfurt force waited for the fog to lift.

German radar picked up LeMay's bombers as they circled over England, and interceptors hit the formation just before the escorting P-47s had to turn back. The German fighters landed and prepared to hound the bombers on the way back to Britain, but the formation instead headed for North Africa. Therefore, when the Schweinfurt mission appeared, some three hours late, the German defenders were armed and ready. After the Allied bombers fought their way into Germany to bomb the ball-bearing factories, the survivors had to face an

During the American capture of Brest, France, in September 1944, bombers attacked fortifications defending the port. The pattern of explosions indicates excellent accuracy.

RIGHT: Armorers load ammunition for the eight .50-caliber guns in the wings of a P-47D, the longer-range, bubble-canopy version of the Republic P-47 Thunderbolt. BELOW: The addition of larger external fuel tanks and, in later models, increased internal fuel capacity, gave the Republic P-47 Thunderbolt the range necessary to escort bombers in Europe and the Pacific.

equally deadly ordeal as they struggled to return to the British Isles.

During the day's battles, German fighters and anti-aircraft fire shot down sixty B-17s in the two formations—one sixth of the bombers that had taken off that morning—and badly damaged twenty-seven others. A total of 601 airmen were killed, captured, or interned in a neutral country. At Regensburg, the bombing proved accurate, but the damage was easily repaired. The raid on Schweinfurt temporarily cut ball-bearing production by 38 percent, but by October output increased beyond the preattack figures.

Although he hit other targets, some during three missions he conducted deep into Germany in a single week, Eaker did not again attack Schweinfurt until October 14, when he dispatched 291 B-17s against the ball-bearing plants there. His losses totaled sixty aircraft shot down and twenty-two damaged beyond repair, but the raid disrupted production, forcing Germany to use substitutes for ball bearings, disperse factories, and import ball bearings from Sweden.

Despite the losses at Schweinfurt, Eaker tried to maintain pressure on German industry with shallow penetrations like the November 2 raid on Emden, when for the first time bombardiers used H2X radar, based on the British H2S. The American version permitted bombing through cloud cover, though less accurately than in clear skies. Arnold, however, had lost patience and replaced Eaker with Doolittle, who took over the Eighth Air Force on January 1, 1944. Spaatz, who had worked closely with Eisenhower in North Africa, accompanied him to the United Kingdom.

Eisenhower became Supreme Commander, Allied Expeditionary Force, and Spaatz commanded the U.S. Strategic Air Forces in Europe, directing the bombing efforts of Doolittle's Eighth Air Force and the Fifteenth, now based in Italy. Eaker went to Italy, where he took command of the Mediterranean Allied Air Forces, with Tedder becoming Eisenhower's deputy commander for air.

The P-51B Mustang

Shortly before Eaker left for the Mediterranean, the airplane he desperately needed, the North American P-51B Mustang, arrived in England. Originally intended to replace the P-40, the P-51 evolved into a deadly high-altitude fighter when fitted with a supercharged Rolls-Royce Merlin liquid-cooled engine. Internal and jettisonable tanks provided enough fuel for missions to Berlin and beyond. The Mustang solved the problem of fighter escort, though too late to keep Eaker in command of the Eighth Air Force.

Armed with the new Mustang fighter and a growing number of bombers, the U.S. Strategic Air Forces again attacked the German aircraft industry. During the Big Week, February 20–25, 1944, the Eighth and the Fifteenth Air Forces launched 3,300 and 500 bomber sorties, respectively, against factories that built aircraft and their components, including the ball-bearing plants at Schweinfurt and Steyr. Thanks in part to 3,500 sorties by long-range fighters, the loss rate for the Big Week was roughly half that for October 1943, when the only escort was the P-47B.

Albert Speer, Hitler's armaments minister, reacted to the attack on aircraft production by at last putting the

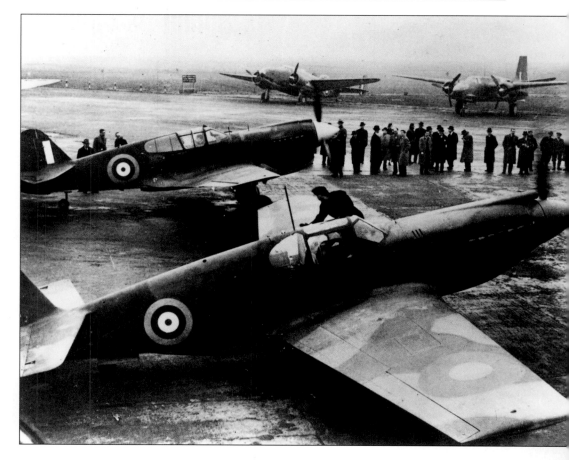

industry on a war footing. He froze designs—though experimental work continued on jets and other aircraft—dispersed production to reduce bomb damage, and expanded the work force, using slave labor when necessary, thus increasing aircraft production. Output rose from 1,300 planes in January 1944, before the Big Week, to 1,600 planes in April and 3,000 in September. This impressive effort could not reverse the tide of war, however, for the United States manufactured twice as many aircraft as Germany's best totals and five times as many engines.

Moreover, the North American training establishment more than made up for casualties, turning out pilots and crewmen who served specific tours. In contrast, the Luftwaffe had a policy of indefinite tours, which could mean serving until killed. In 1943, Germany lost 35,000 pilots and crewmen compared to the 49,000 on duty when the year began. Only the best or the luckiest survived to fly the planes Speer was building.

North American Aviation designed the fighter that became the Mustang as a replacement for the Curtiss P-40. Mustang I, powered like the P-40, by an Allison engine, proved fast and agile but only at low altitudes. The substitution of a supercharged Rolls-Royce Merlin engine converted the P-51B into a first-line fighter with six .50-caliber machine guns and range enough for missions to Berlin. The Allison-powered version became the A-36 dive-bomber.

Machines and Men

After replacing Eaker in command of the Eighth Air Force, Doolittle benefitted not only from the P-51B, and from new versions of the P-47 and P-38, but from a miracle of aircraft production.

U.S. factories produced slightly more than 26,000 airplanes in 1941, almost 48,000 in 1942, and in excess of 96,000 in the peak year of 1944. Harris relied on a smaller British production base that exceeded 20,000 in 1941 and peaked at 26,000. The United States and Great Britain turned out almost 19,000 bombers in 1942 and dropped 53,000 tons (47,700t) of bombs on Europe. Anglo-American production of bombers reached 37,083 in 1943, 42,906 in 1944, and 23,554 during 1945 before the war ended. The weight of bombs dropped on Europe in the corresponding periods was 226,513 tons (203,862t), 1,186,000 tons (1,067,400t), and 477,051 tons (429,346t).

To maintain production required a work force that peaked at 2 million in the United States and 1.6 million in Great Britain. Both nations made extensive use of women workers, and the United States mastered the assembly line, where complicated tasks were broken down into simple, repetitious actions that an unskilled person could perform. By ensuring profits, cutting taxes, building factories for lease to manufacturers, and timing orders to avoid slack time, the United States increased factory floor space devoted to aircraft manufacture from 25.4 million square feet (65.8 square m) in 1941 to 165.7 million square feet (429.2 square m) at the end of 1944.

As the inventory of aircraft grew, the United States was also mass-producing pilots and aircrews at new bases bulldozed out of farmland and desert. Allied airmen from as far away as China and Great Britain trained in the American South and Southwest. Indeed, the Army Air Forces had a surplus of trainees at the end of 1944 and transferred some of them to the Ground Forces and Service Forces. Women also entered the military manpower pool, serving as combat pilots in the Soviet Union, performing clerical and other noncombat duties for Britain, Canada, and the United States, and delivering aircraft and other noncombat flying for the U.S. Army Air Forces.

As early as the spring of 1942, the North American aircraft industry had begun employing women, such as these propeller inspectors. In the United States, Canada, the United Kingdom, and the Soviet Union, women formed an important part of the work force and also served as pilots, flying combat missions for the Soviet air arm.

LEFT, TOP: The acceleration of German fighter production in 1944, under the direction of Albert Speer, came too late, as demonstrated by the wreckage of these Me 109s destroyed on the ground. The oil offensive rapidly choked off the fuel needed to train pilots for the aircraft that Speer's reforms, including use of slave labor, had built. LEFT, BOTTOM: The inability to train enough pilots also handicapped the jet-fighter force, including the Me 262, potentially the deadliest of World War II interceptors. Introduction of the revolutionary fighter was delayed by difficulty in developing a reliable engine and, to a lesser degree, by Hitler's indecision regarding whether to use the jet as a hit-and-run bomber or interceptor.

Bombing Berlin

Although Harris, during Big Week, sent Bomber Command against five cities involved in aircraft or ball-bearing manufacture, he concentrated on bombing Berlin. Late in 1943 he had told Churchill that "We can wreck Berlin from end to end if the USAAF [U.S. Army Air Forces] will come in on it. It will cost us between 400 and 500 bombers. It will cost Germany the war."

Spaatz believed that destroying industries, rather than leveling the capital, held the key to victory. Not until March 4 did the Eighth Air Force attempt to attack a target in Berlin. Because of cloud cover, that strike was recalled, but twenty-nine bombers failed to hear the order and dropped their bombs. Three additional strikes between March 6 and March 22 hit factories in Berlin and its suburbs, encountering clouds and determined resistance. On March 6, for example, the defenders downed 69 of 672 bombers.

Harris raided Berlin sixteen times between August 1943 and March 24, 1944. Bomber Command lost more than 1,100 bombers to revived air defenses that made extensive use of Tame Boar night fighters. Since the introduction of Window, rigid control boxes no longer existed. Instead controllers helped the interceptors locate the bomber stream; afterward the fighter crews relied on their airborne radar and any ambient light to find victims.

Especially deadly were the twin-engine night fighters fitted with upward-firing 20mm cannons that enabled the crew to locate a bomber from its exhaust flame or its bulk, fly underneath, and silhouette the victim against the lighter sky. Not only did Bomber Command lose twice as many bombers as Harris had predicted, but Berlin still functioned as capital, and Germany continued fighting.

The ordeal of the Battle of Berlin had barely ended when Harris attacked Nuremberg, Bomber Command's costliest raid of the war. On the night of March 30, 1944, 779 Halifaxes and Lancasters took off for the early morning attack. The Germans succeeded in tracking the H2S radar that the pathfinders used for navigation, and a bright moon favored the defenders, who shot down ninety-three bombers. Two others collided in midair, and another ten crashed in England near the end of the return

LEFT: Eighth Air Force bombers, including this B-17G, attacked Nuremberg in February 1945, bombing through cloud cover. By this time, most German cities had suffered damage that leveled many of the man-made structures that might have served the Americans as aiming points, thus undermining still further the accuracy of daylight bombing. BELOW: Repeated aerial bombing battered Nuremberg to rubble, but a statue of Albrecht Durer, the medieval artist, somehow escaped destruction.

Germany's Vengeance Weapons

Besides developing the twin-turbojet Me 262, which appeared in April 1944, and the rocket-powered Me 163 interceptor, which entered service in July 1944, Germany developed two vengeance weapons, the V-1 flying bomb and the V-2 rocket, designed to avenge the Anglo-American bombing offensive.

British Flight Officer Constance Babington-Smith, a photo interpreter, spotted a V-1 on pictures taken by a reconnaissance plane over the Baltic island of Peenemunde, and Lancasters attacked on the night of August 17, 1943, delaying the work there. By year's end, however, aerial photographs of western Europe began revealing oddly shaped structures that photo interpreters associated with the V-1 and V-2.

Between December 1943 and June 1944, tactical and strategic aircraft dropped some 36,000 tons (32,400t) of bombs on the installations, but the enemy nevertheless succeeded in launching its first "buzz bomb," on June 13, 1944, and his first V-2 on September 8. The two weapons killed almost 9,000 in London alone, and the rain of explosives lasted until ground forces overran the launch sites at the end of March 1945.

The Messerschmitt Me 163 rocket-powered interceptor climbed to the altitude of the bomber formation, made one firing pass with its cannon, and then glided to earth. If any of the highly volatile fuel remained on board, a hard landing could result in a fatal explosion.

flight. The bombing proved inaccurate, and the damage was light.

Before the Battle of Berlin ended, Spaatz proposed a systematic attack on oil refineries and synthetic fuel plants, arguing that their destruction would bring Hitler to his knees. Harris objected that no single "panacea target," whether ball bearings or oil, could ensure victory; only methodical attacks on cities and their inhabitants would win the war. The Allied high command considered oil an important target but doubted that production could be halted in time to affect the impending invasion of France and wanted the strategic bombers to paralyze the enemy's transportation.

On the advice of Arnold, Spaatz directed the Fifteenth Air Force to hit the rail yards at Ploesti, knowing that bombs would explode among the refineries. The Fifteenth Air Force struck on April 5, 1944, disrupting oil production and encouraging Spaatz to attack again on April 15 and 24. Depending on Eaker to maintain pressure on the oil industry with the Foggia-based bombers, Spaatz persuaded Eisenhower to allow Doolittle to attack synthetic oil plants. On May 12, 800 Eighth Air Force bombers raided 8 facilities, losing 46 bombers and 10 fighters. Ultra soon revealed that the Germans were conserving fuel and shifting antiaircraft batteries to protect the vital industry.

Shuttle Bombing

On June 2 Eaker inaugurated a program of shuttle bombing, leading bombers from Italy to the Soviet Union, attacking transportation targets en route, and bombing an airfield from Soviet bases before hitting another airfield on June 11 while returning to Italy.

Shuttle bombing continued after the invasion of Normandy on June 6. An Eighth Air Force mission bombed a synthetic fuel plant near Berlin on June 21, then landed at airfields in the Ukraine. A German reconnaissance plane shadowed the bombers bound for Poltava, and that night an air raid destroyed forty-three B-17s and fifteen P-51Ds, the latter type of plane being a greatly improved version of the Mustang.

As Allied armies converged on Germany, use of the vulnerable Soviet bases declined in importance, and the American use of such fields as Poltava ended during September, after Soviet authorities withheld permission for the shuttle missions to drop supplies to anticommunist Polish resistance fighters in Warsaw.

Allied Domination of the Skies

The strategic purpose of the Combined Bomber Offensive yielded in the spring of 1944 to Operation Overlord as the heavy bombers joined tactical aircraft in attacking the coastal defenses of Normandy.

Planners also intended to use the B-17s and B-24s to destroy bridges and viaducts, but Spaatz protested diverting strategic bombers to tactical targets, and a test mission flown by Martin B-26 medium bombers and P-47 fighter-bombers damaged three bridges from low altitude and destroyed a fourth. By D-Day, June 6, tactical aircraft had dropped every bridge across the Seine, preventing German troops from advancing beyond the river.

Besides hampering reinforcement of Normandy's defenses, Allied aircraft so dominated the skies over the invasion beaches that the Luftwaffe managed just 100 sorties on D-Day to oppose some 8,000 Allied aircraft. The aerial armada included the transports that dropped paratroops and released gliders in the early morning darkness of D-Day. The airborne troops were scattered because of cloud cover and antiaircraft fire, but during the day, the airborne and amphibious soldiers made contact.

After heavy bombers helped secure the beachhead (for example, Lancasters collapsed a railroad tunnel leading into Normandy), they helped engineer a breakout. On July 7 and 18 Montgomery resorted to carpet bombing to crack the defenses around Caen. At St. Lô on July 25, 1,500 B-17s and B-24s pounded the German lines. Unfortunately, stray bombs killed or wounded 102 Americans. When the enemy counterattacked at Mortain after the St. Lô breakthrough, Ultra gave warning and fighter-bombers pounced on the German armor as it advanced.

LEFT: An Italian-based Consolidated B-24 Liberator, its right wing badly damaged, limps over Toulon, France, during a raid on June 8, 1944. BELOW: Flares and antiaircraft fire illuminate the airfield at Poltava in the Soviet Ukraine in the early hours of June 22, 1944, as German aircraft attack the shuttle-bombing B-17s and P-51s that had arrived on the previous day.

The Ilyushin Il-2 Stormovik, the deadliest attack plane of World War II, had armor to protect it from light antiaircraft weapons as it supported the Soviet advance with bombs, rockets, cannons, and machine guns.

The Allies also controlled the skies over southern France, where amphibious and airborne troops landed on the Riviera coast on August 15. The Luftwaffe sank an LST, or Landing Ship Tank, a craft specially designed to disgorge armored vehicles over a ramp in the bow, and damaged a command ship before withdrawing inland because of Allied aerial might. American tactical aircraft preyed upon the columns retreating up the Rhône valley, destroying an estimated 1,400 trucks, 30 locomotives, and 263 railway cars. Early in September, the troops advancing from the Riviera and those from the Normandy beaches met to form one continuous front.

The Allies attempted to use the First Allied Airborne Army, which Brereton now commanded, to outflank the defenses of the Ruhr by landing beyond the Rhine at Arnhem, Holland. On September 17, 1,500 transports and gliders, escorted by 1,300 fighters, landed some 20,000 troops at Arnhem and along the highway leading there. The armored force that was to advance along the highway got bogged down far short of Arnhem, even though 250 B-24s dropped supplies to the American troops holding the key bridges. Arnhem had to be abandoned.

The Oil Campaign

Meanwhile, the oil campaign had resumed, with the participation of Bomber Command. Harris never lost his distrust of panacea targets, such as oil production, thinking it unreasonable to believe when it began that the campaign would succeed, but he later conceded that

"Allied strategists . . . bet on an outsider, and it happened to win." Harris's Lancasters and Halifaxes, with a greater bomb capacity than the B-17s and B-24s, dropped 40 percent of the total tonnage during the oil campaign, most of it after November 1944.

Soviet armies, supported by new aircraft from an industry that in 1944 matched Nazi Germany in output, contributed to the oil offensive by overrunning Ploesti in August 1944, freeing the Fifteenth Air Force to attack synthetic fuel plants throughout southeastern Europe. The resulting fuel shortage cut pilot training and made it difficult to man the aircraft Speer was rapidly manufacturing.

Although fuel supplies were dwindling, Germany husbanded enough to counterattack from the Ardennes on December 16, 1944, triggering the Battle of the Bulge. Since the enemy could rely on telephone and teletype, Ultra provided no warning, and Allied intelligence interpreted the unusual activity preceding the counterattack as preparations to withdraw. Allied air power intervened after the cloud cover parted on December 23, but wind and snow on the last three days of the year again impeded aerial operations.

Until the elimination of the salient on January 28, 1945, heavy bombers and tactical aircraft hammered the bulge and the lines of supply that sustained it.

A Death Knell for Nazi Germany

On January 1, as the Battle of the Bulge raged, the Luftwaffe made a desperate effort to seize the initiative in the west. Almost 900 planes hit Allied bases in Belgium, France, and Holland, squandering fuel and 300 airplanes to destroy 150 easily replaced aircraft. Strict secrecy frustrated Ultra, but it also caused German antiaircraft gunners, who assumed that so many airplanes had to be Allied, to fire on their own formations, not knowing that the Luftwaffe was again in action.

While the oil offensive and the bombing of Berlin continued, the Anglo-American Allies tried to destroy the German transportation system, attacking targets spared thus far, such as Dresden. This city stood astride a rail line the Germans could use to escape the Red

Army just 70 miles (112km) away. Lightly bombed, most of its aircraft batteries transferred elsewhere, Dresden attracted a series of devastating attacks out of proportion to its military importance. On the night of February 13 Bomber Command ignited a firestorm that rivaled the conflagration at Hamburg in deaths and destruction. American daylight bombers followed up, attacking the rail yard on February 14 and 15 and again on April 17.

Operation Varsity, the final airborne operation of the war, took place on March 24, 1945, in conjunction with the crossing of the Rhine near Wesel. Allied domination of the air prevented the remnants of Germany's surviving fighter force from interfering with Varsity, but several transports were downed or damaged by intense antiaircraft fire. Soviet troops captured Berlin—where Hitler committed suicide on April 30 in his fortified bunker—then linked up with the western Allies, while the soldiers that had landed on the Riviera met the Allied troops that had overrun Italy. Nazi Germany surrendered at Rheims, France, on May 7.

ABOVE: In 1945, Berlin became a frequent target for as many as a thousand aircraft like this B-17G. When carrying a large proportion of incendiaries and salvoing their loads without using aiming points, the attackers erased any remaining difference in accuracy between daylight and night bombing. LEFT: British and American bombs and Soviet artillery had gutted Potsdam, a city near Berlin, by the time Germany surrendered.

Chapter 7

Triumph in the Pacific

WHEN THE COUNTEROFFENSIVE AGAINST JAPAN BEGAN IN THE SUMMER OF 1942, air power played a key role, but not the one predicted by Air Corps strategic-bombing enthusiasts. There were too few heavy bombers in the far Pacific and, despite the base the Japanese were developing at Rabaul, New Britain, not enough strategic targets within range. B-17s and B-24s proved valuable for long-range reconnaissance, however, and attacking shipping.

The New Guinea Campaign

Although Adm. Chester W. Nimitz, in command of the Pacific Ocean areas, sent a carrier task force against New Britain and New Guinea during March 1942, he remained wary of entrusting the valuable ships to the theater commander, a U.S. Army officer, Gen. MacArthur. Only once during the New Guinea fighting, when the Allies attacked Hollandia in April 1944, did the fast carriers support MacArthur's operations there. As a result, until escort carriers joined the Seventh Fleet shortly before the Hollandia landing, MacArthur had to rely on U.S. Army and Australian aircraft to gain control of the skies, forming and enlarging an aerial umbrella beneath which his troops advanced.

During the early fighting on New Guinea, the Douglas C-47 defied mountains and jungles to deliver men and cargo and evacuate the wounded. Maj. Gen. George Kenney—commanding

LEFT: Jubilant after having downed seventeen Japanese planes over the Gilbert Islands, U.S. Navy pilots pose by the tail of a Grumman F6F Hellcat on board the new USS *Lexington*, namesake of the aircraft carrier lost in the Battle of the Coral Sea.

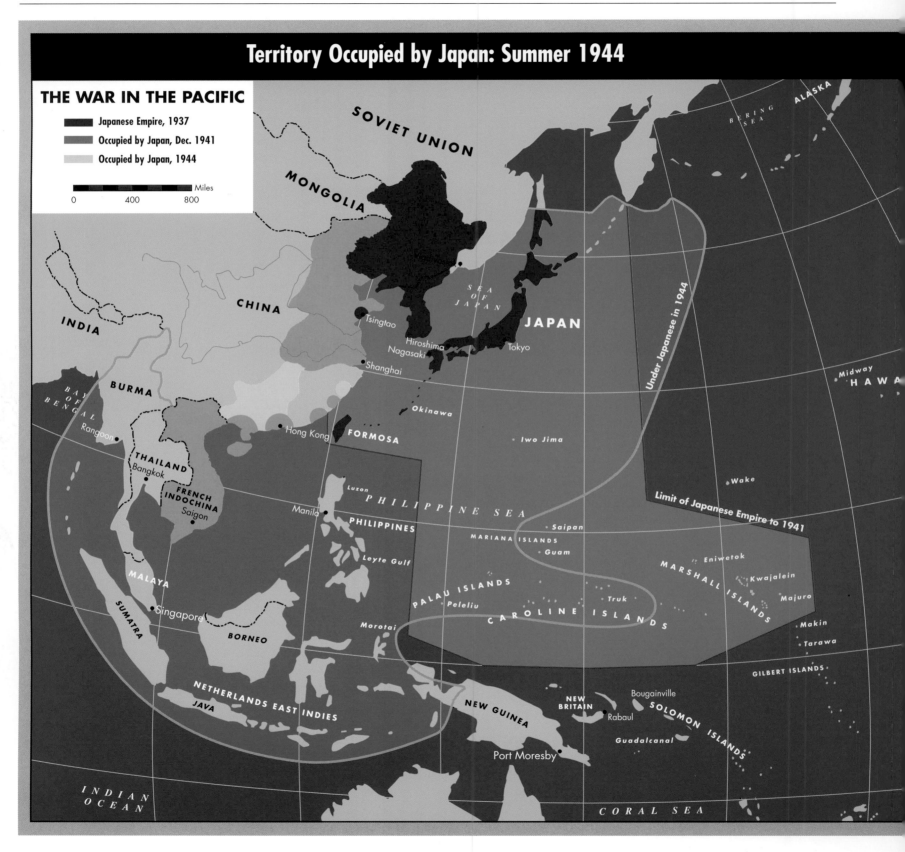

Territory Occupied by Japan: Summer 1944

THE WAR IN THE PACIFIC

- Japanese Empire, 1937
- Occupied by Japan, Dec. 1941
- Occupied by Japan, 1944

Miles
0   400   800

SOVIET UNION

ALASKA

BERING SEA

MONGOLIA

CHINA

INDIA

SEA OF JAPAN

JAPAN

Tsingtao

Hiroshima
Nagasaki

Tokyo

Shanghai

Midway

HAWA

BAY OF BENGAL

BURMA

Okinawa

Rangoon

Hong Kong

FORMOSA

Iwo Jima

THAILAND

Bangkok

FRENCH INDOCHINA

Saigon

Luzon

Manila

PHILIPPINE SEA

Wake

Under Japanese in 1944

PHILIPPINES

Leyte Gulf

Saipan

MARIANA ISLANDS

Guam

Limit of Japanese Empire to 1941

Eniwetok

MARSHALL ISLANDS

Kwajalein

MALAYA

Majuro

SUMATRA

Singapore

BORNEO

Morotai

PALAU ISLANDS

Peleliu

Truk

CAROLINE ISLANDS

Makin

Tarawa

NETHERLANDS EAST INDIES

JAVA

GILBERT ISLANDS

NEW GUINEA

Bougainville

NEW BRITAIN

Rabaul

SOLOMON ISLANDS

Guadalcanal

Port Moresby

INDIAN OCEAN

CORAL SEA

LEFT: The Central Pacific campaign, supported by carrier aircraft and a few land-based bombers, projected U.S. amphibious forces through the Gilberts and Marshalls to the Marianas, where Seabees and U.S. Army engineers built bases from which B-29s could bomb Japan. The conquest of Saipan in the Mariana Islands toppled the government of Japanese Prime Minister Hideki Tojo, who clearly saw the handwriting on the wall and resigned.

Control of the sea lanes enabled the United States to sustain B-29 operations from the Marianas, whereas a B-29 offensive from China failed because of a tenuous supply line and the inability of Chinese forces to protect the airfields. U.S. submarines had in the meantime cut off Japan from its sources of fuel and other war materials. Nevertheless, Japan's rulers persisted in the increasingly hopeless struggle until shocked into surrender by two atomic bombs.

general of the U.S. Fifth Air Force and the Allied air commander for the Southwest Pacific—also had P-39s, an export version of the P-39 known as the P-400, and P-40s, as well as B-17s, A-20s, and B-25s. Maj. Paul I. Gunn fitted some B-25s with a solid nose mounting eight machine guns for strafing. When another solid-nose B-25 mounting a 75mm howitzer arrived in the theater, Gunn added four forward-firing machine guns to complement the powerful but slow-firing cannon.

As MacArthur's troops took the offensive, B-24s joined the B-17s, and P-38s and P-47s became the standard fighters, aided, beginning in 1944, by the twin-engine, twin-boom Northrop P-61 Black Widow night fighter. Strafing versions of the B-25 shot up Japanese airfields, and other B-25s cratered runways with delayed-action bombs. The A-20s dropped para-chute fragmentation bombs on parked airplanes, and a handful of B-26s joined in the attacks. The C-47s

ABOVE: A North American B-25 Mitchell bombs a Japanese merchantman during a raid on Rabaul, New Britain. Allied amphibious forces seized much of New Britain but relied on air power to neutralize Rabaul, which remained in the hands of the Japanese.

A ground crew loads 250-pound (110kg) bombs for a training mission. This type of aircraft, and the PBJ version flown by the U.S. Navy and Marine Corps, bombed bypassed Japanese bases other than Rabaul throughout the Pacific.

dropped Australian and American paratroops at Nadzab in September 1943, and in July 1944, with New Guinea essentially secure, the transports dropped some 1,500 Americans at Noemfoor, an island off the northwest coast.

The greatest aerial victory of the New Guinea campaign came in the Bismarck Sea during March 1944, after the cryptanalysts at Pearl Harbor learned that a Japanese convoy would sail from Rabaul with reinforcements for New Guinea. American and Australian aircraft attacked—the B-25s proving especially deadly dropping delayed-action bombs from mast-head height—sinking

a dozen of the 16 ships on March 2 and 3 and killing 3,000 Japanese soldiers.

Guadalcanal and the Solomons Campaign

Another counteroffensive began in the Solomon Islands on August 7, 1942, when the 1st Marine Division landed at Guadalcanal, Gavutu, and Tulagi.

The carrier task force supporting the landing withdrew to safer waters, exposing the transports to air attack and causing them to steam away with cargo still on board. The division commander, Maj. Gen. Alexander A. Vandegrift, later declared that his marines, short on supplies from the outset, were "bare ass" before Japanese air and naval might.

The carriers *Saratoga*, *Wasp*, and *Enterprise* returned later in August to help blunt a Japanese attempt to neutralize the Marine airfield on Guadalcanal, bring in reinforcements, and provoke a naval battle. *Saratoga* launched a strike that fatally damaged the light carrier *Ryujo* and sank some lesser ships. As the destroyer *Mitsuki* stopped to rescue troops from a sinking transport, B-17s from the New Hebrides sent the warship to the ocean bottom. In return, before the Guadalcanal campaign ended in February 1943, the Japanese sank both *Wasp* and *Hornet*.

During the critical months of the battle for Guadalcanal, Marine airmen, reinforced by U.S. Army squadrons and occasionally by U.S. Navy carrier aircraft that had landed for fuel, provided air cover from a

captured airstrip named Henderson Field in honor of Maj. Lofton Henderson, a Marine dive-bomber pilot killed at Midway. Because the F4Fs flown by the marines performed better at high altitude than the U.S. Army's P-400s, Army airmen supported troops on the ground, while marines tangled with Japanese bombers and fighters.

The Guadalcanal campaign produced fighter aces like Maj. Gregory Boyington (a former Flying Tiger), Capt. Joseph J. Foss, and Maj. Robert E. Galer, but other pilots made their own contributions. On November 13, marine dive-bombers and torpedo bombers joined Navy aircraft staging through Henderson Field in crippling the battleship *Hiei*, already damaged by naval gunfire, which was then scuttled.

As the Guadalcanal campaign ended, U.S. Army P-38s reached the island. On April 18, 1943, the anniversary of the Halsey-Doolittle raid, a flight of these long-range fighters shot down a bomber carrying

ABOVE: Gregory Boyington, a former Flying Tiger, was the leading Marine Corps ace in the Pacific when shot down by the Japanese and taken prisoner. He survived forced labor and received the Medal of Honor from President Harry S. Truman in recognition of his aerial exploits. LEFT: In December 1942, Marine SBD dive-bombers warm up at primitive Henderson Field on Guadalcanal to attack the Japanese forces that would withdraw from the island in February 1943.

ABOVE: Flown by marines and naval airmen, the Vought F4U Corsair proved equally effective whether using its six .50-caliber machine guns to tangle with Japanese aircraft or dropping bombs and napalm in support of troops.

Admiral Yamamoto, architect of the Pearl Harbor attack, who died in the crash. Nimitz's code-breakers had discovered the schedule of an inspection trip, enabling the fighters to spring an ambush at Bougainville.

From Guadalcanal, the counteroffensive moved into the central and northern Solomons. At this juncture, Marine airmen acquired the Chance Vought F4U Corsair, a fighter vastly superior to the older Grumman, and an unsuccessful night fighter version of the Lockheed PV-1 patrol bomber, which lacked speed and ceiling. The Solomons campaign ended on November 1, 1943, when marines landed on Bougainville to establish a perimeter, though the Japanese there resisted until the end of the war.

The Quebec Conference

Allied strategists originally pictured eastern New Guinea and the Solomons as the pincers that would crush Rabaul, but the Quebec Conference of August 1943 ended with an agreement to bypass Rabaul rather than capture it. MacArthur would advance from New Guinea to the Philippines, and the marines would seize most of New Britain, isolating Rabaul, which aerial bombardment would neutralize, even though the base would remain in Japanese hands.

The Allied leaders meeting at Quebec also addressed the use of the Boeing B-29. The Anglo-American Combined Chiefs of Staff—including Leahy, King, Marshall, and Arnold—not only decided to attack Japan from airfields in China but also approved an offensive in the Central Pacific, which would ultimately seize islands in the Mariana Islands within B-29 range of Japan.

The Central Pacific Campaign

The Central Pacific campaign began at Tarawa and Makin Atolls in the Gilbert Islands on November 22, 1943. The invading soldiers methodically overran fortified but lightly held Makin, but on November 24 a Japanese submarine sank the escort carrier *Liscome Bay*, which was supporting the operation.

Tarawa proved to be both heavily fortified and tenaciously defended. The preparatory naval gunfire and air strikes were less effective than planned, and the Japanese fought to the death—the attacking marines captured only 17 wounded defenders and 129 Korean laborers.

Throughout the Central Pacific drive, the U.S. Navy made use of a new single-engine, single-seat fighter, the Grumman F6F Hellcat, which replaced the smaller F4F Wildcat early in 1943. The Grumman TBF torpedo bombers, a few of which fought at Midway, had supplanted the lumbering TBDs. Delayed by development problems, the Curtiss SB2C Helldiver did not begin replacing the SBD until late 1943. Besides acquiring escort carriers built on tanker or freighter hulls (which eventually totaled 110, thirty-three of them on loan to the British), the Navy was commissioning nine 11,000-ton (9,900t) Independence-class light carriers, built on light-cruiser hulls, and two dozen 27,100-ton (24,390t) Essex-class fast carriers.

Improved preparatory naval gunfire and air strikes neutralized the most dangerous defenses facing the amphibious forces that landed at Kwajalein and Majuro Atolls in the Marshall Islands on January 31, 1944, and at Eniwetok Atoll on February 17. Simultaneously with the invasion of Eniwetok, United States carrier aircraft attacked Truk, formerly a major base of Japan's Combined Fleet but now an anchorage for light warships and merchantmen.

At Truk, planes from Vice Adm. Marc Mitscher's Task Force 58 shot down 275 Japanese planes while sinking 3 light cruisers, 4 destroyers, and some 200,000 tons (180,000t) of merchant shipping. The attackers lost twenty-five planes, and the fast carrier *Intrepid* sustained damage from an aerial torpedo. While the war moved into the Mariana Islands, U.S. aircraft neutralized Truk and other bypassed strongholds in the Marshalls and Carolines.

The Mariana Islands

In the Marianas, amphibious forces attacked three large islands in succession—Saipan on June 15, 1944, Guam on July 21, and Tinian on July 24 in a shore-to-shore operation from Saipan, each requiring from one to three weeks of fighting.

On June 22, the first of seventy-three P-47 Thunderbolts flew ashore at Saipan from an escort carrier. They strafed, fired rockets, and dropped half-ton (.45t) bombs and napalm to help U.S. Navy pilots support operations on the three islands. Marine fighters and torpedo bombers saw action on Guam, where Marine F6F night fighters took over from Saipan-based Army P-61s. Marine observation planes and radar operators saw action on all three islands.

The most spectacular aerial action occurred over the Philippine Sea. A Japanese fleet, under Vice Adm. Jisaburo Ozawa, sortied to defend the Marianas; his forces included 3 large carriers—*Taiho*, *Shokaku*, and *Zuikaku*—and 5 smaller ones, for an aggregate of 450 planes. Mitscher's Task Force 58, with 902 aircraft divided among 15 carriers, returned from attacking airfields in the Bonins in time to give battle.

The Boeing B-29 Superfortress

Described by General Arnold as a $3 billion gamble, the Boeing B-29 incorporated such advanced technology as a pressurized cabin, remotely controlled gun turrets, and wing flaps that could increase the lifting surface by 20 percent. The new bomber had a top speed in excess of 300 miles per hour (480kph), a range of more than 5,000 miles (8,000km), and a ceiling of 30,000 feet (9,150m).

However, the B-29's four 2,200-horsepower, twin-row radial engines tended from the outset to overheat. Indeed, one of the test aircraft caught fire and crashed, killing all on board and twenty persons on the ground. Design changes that increased the flow of air around the second row of cylinders improved cooling, but engine reliability remained a problem when the bombers entered combat. The B-29 nevertheless set fire to much of urban Japan and dropped the two atomic bombs.

The Boeing B-29 Superfortress symbolized the collaborative nature of the war against Japan, in which the U.S. Navy projected Army and Marine Corps forces some 3,000 miles to seize bases in the Mariana Islands from which the Superfortresses could pound Japan.

LEFT: Mitsubishi G4M bombers, nicknamed Betty by Allied airmen, bore through antiaircraft fire to attack shipping off Guadalcanal.

RIGHT: Standing in the waist of a B-17, Gen. Douglas MacArthur observes the dropping of American paratroops in New Guinea during 1943.

RIGHT: The Northrop P-61 Black Widow, the first American aircraft designed expressly as a night fighter, rivaled the B-25 in size but was faster and more maneuverable.

LEFT: Navy Fighting Squadron VF 17, commanded by Lt. Comdr. John T. Blackburn, stands at attention while Marine Gen. Ralph J. Mitchell, air commander in the Solomons, presents a unit citation.

The *Kamikaze*

The name *kamikaze*, or "divine wind," recalled the storm that in 1281 scattered a Mongol fleet and saved Japan from invasion. The modern kamikaze corps was intended to duplicate this feat by diving into American ships, trading one life for many, and ultimately shatter American morale, forcing the United States to let Japan survive.

Military and economic reality motivated the decision to call for volunteers to die for emperor and country. American submarines were sinking tankers carrying oil from the Netherlands East Indies, forcing Japan to experiment with alcohol as a fuel extender. Even so, the nation ended 1944 with only 1.5 million barrels of low-octane gasoline, compared to the 4.2-million-barrel stockpile of high-octane fuel on hand in December 1941. Moreover, many of the most experienced Japanese pilots had died at Midway, in the Solomons, or in the Marianas Turkey Shoot. Their replacements received minimal training because of the fuel shortage, logging perhaps 100 hours, compared to 300 in 1941. A kamikaze, however, would need perhaps fifteen hours of flight training.

BELOW, TOP: A Japanese dive-bomber plunges through antiaircraft fire toward the aircraft carrier *Hornet*, a veteran of the Halsey-Doolittle raid, during the Battle of Santa Cruz in October 1942. BELOW, BOTTOM: Either deliberately or because of flak damage, the plane crashes into the carrier and explodes, inflicting mortal damage. RIGHT: Crew members of the aircraft carrier *Intrepid*, nicknamed the Evil Eye, fight the blaze ignited on April 16, 1945, when a kamikaze crashed into the flight deck.

Ozawa's scout planes spotted Mitscher's ships on June 18, and the Japanese planned to attack on the following morning. An American patrol bomber sighted Ozawa early on June 19, but the report went astray. Mitscher's radar later revealed, however, that 374 Japanese aircraft were headed toward the task force. The resulting air battle, known as the Marianas Turkey Shoot, claimed 244 Japanese planes launched from carriers and 50 based on the islands. F6Fs shot down 275 at the cost of 31 Hellcats, and antiaircraft fire downed the other 19 planes. During the Turkey Shoot, American submarines sank *Taiho* and *Shokaku.*

Late on the afternoon of June 20, Task Force 58 located the enemy and launched a strike. Ozawa proved farther away than reported, however, and daylight was fading when the Americans pounced, shooting down eighty Japanese planes but losing seventeen while sinking one small carrier and damaging four others, sinking two oilers, and damaging several other ships. By nightfall, just 47 of the 450 airplanes that Ozawa had brought into battle survived. As the victorious Americans returned, short of fuel, Mitscher ordered his ships to turn on searchlights to guide them back, ignoring the danger from submarines. Despite the illumination, forty-nine pilots and crewmen failed to return.

Bombing Japan From China

On June 15, 1944, D-Day at Saipan, B-29s flying from China bombed a steel mill at Yawata, Japan, inflicting minor damage, but contrary to American expectations, signaling a winding down of the air war in China. The raid was conducted by the XX Bomber Command of the Twentieth Air Force. Arnold, as the executive agent of the Joint Chiefs of Staff, exercised overall command of the Twentieth Air Force from Washington, D.C.

The severing of the Burma Road in 1942 had forced the Allies to fly all supplies over the Himalayas, known as the Hump, until the opening of the Ledo Road in January 1945. C-47s had pioneered the air route, joined by the larger Curtiss C-46, two variants of the B-24, the C-87 transport and the gasoline-carrying C-109 tanker. The monthly deliveries they made to China increased from 1,500 tons (1,350t) in January 1943 to 4,000 (3,600t) in November 1943 and 30,000 (27,000t) in December 1944. Even so, this tonnage could not support the Chinese army, Chennault's air operations, and the B-29s, although the bombers shuttled fuel and munitions from India.

Maj. Gen Kenneth B. Wolfe, who had helped develop the B-29, led the XX Bomber Command, but he could not amass the resources for the sustained bombing of Japan. As he had with Eaker, Arnold lost patience and replaced Wolfe with LeMay, who drilled his crews in the high-altitude tactics used in Europe.

Although LeMay improved bombing accuracy and used incendiaries to devastate the waterfront at Japanese-held Hankow, China, he could not overcome the problems of supply. In January 1945, with Japanese forces threatening the airfields in China, LeMay left China for the Marianas, and the B-29s passed under the control of Lord Louis Mountbatten, of Great Britain, the nonflying Allied supreme commander in India, who used them for bombing and mine-laying purposes in Southeast Asia.

During the B-29 campaign from China, Brig. Gen. Haywood S. Hansell, in command of the XXI Bomber Command of the Twentieth Air Force, arrived in the Marianas and launched the first strike from bases there on November 24, 1944. Over Japan, Hansell's crews encountered frequent cloud cover and jet stream winds that could propel the B-29s over the target at 400 miles per hour (640kph), disrupting bombing patterns. The early attacks damaged the aircraft industry, however, and in doing so struck a symbolic blow against Tokyo. Following orders from Washington, Hansell used incendiaries to start destructive fires at Nagoya, but Arnold decided that LeMay, who took over on January 20, 1945, could do a better job. Having sent LeMay to replace Wolfe in China, Arnold now chose LeMay to replace Hansell in the Marianas.

Leyte and the Philippines

While the bombing of Japan proceeded, MacArthur redeemed the pledge he had made to return to the Philippines, seizing Morotai Island on September 15, 1945, as a stepping stone.

On that same day, marines and soldiers landed at Peleliu and Angaur in the Palau Islands to protect MacArthur's eastern flank. MacArthur's troops invaded the Philippine island of Leyte on October 20, spurring the Japanese to risk the remnants of their navy and to unleash a new weapon, the kamikaze.

The Japanese navy made a three-pronged response to the invasion of Leyte. Admiral Ozawa was to approach from the north and lure Halsey's fast carriers and battleships away from the island; the bait consisted of four aircraft carriers and two converted battleships with flight decks replacing their aft turrets. Two other forces would converge on Leyte: one through Surigao Strait; and the other, commanded by Vice Adm. Takeo Kurita, through San Bernardino Strait. Kurita's force included the world's two largest battleships, *Musashi* and *Yamato*.

Two United States submarines sighted Kurita, sank two of his cruisers, and reported his position to Halsey, whose scout planes confirmed the sighting on the morning of October 24. Before the American admiral could launch a strike, 180 land-based aircraft attacked him. Although Comdr. David McCampbell, who downed nine planes, and his fellow pilots slaughtered these Japanese, a separate attack set fires on the light carrier *Princeton*

ABOVE: Adm. William F. Halsey, Jr., commander of the Third Fleet at the Battle of Leyte Gulf, displayed an aggressiveness rooted in the daring April 1942 bombing of Japan, when he commanded the task force that brought Jimmy Doolittle's B-25s within striking distance of the Home Islands. OPPOSITE: A Japanese dive-bomber, set ablaze by antiaircraft fire, streaks beyond the escort carrier *Kitkin Bay* and crashes into the sea.

ABOVE: Grumman F6F Hellcat fighters warm up on the flight deck of the aircraft carrier *Bunker Hill* off Saipan in June 1944. Curtiss SB2C Helldiver dive-bombers wait at the far end of the deck. RIGHT: A three-place Grumman TBF Avenger torpedo plane returns to its carrier after an attack that set fire to Japanese installations on Marcus Island. Former U.S. President George Bush flew this kind of aircraft while a naval aviator in the Pacific during World War II.

OPPOSITE: Grumman TBF torpedo planes (foreground) and Curtiss SB2C Helldiver dive-bombers conduct horizontal bombing against Hokodate, Japan, as the war draws toward an end.

When high-altitude, daylight precision strikes against military and industrial targets proved ineffectual, in part because of jet-stream winds that scattered the bombs, LeMay switched to low-altitude fire raids by night and by day that burned entire cities.

that detonated a magazine, sinking the first United States carrier lost since *Hornet* in 1942. As the explosion rocked *Princeton*, some 250 of Halsey's planes hit Kurita, sinking *Musashi*.

The thrust through Surigao Strait ended in a surface battle that sank or drove off all the Japanese ships involved. Halsey learned of Ozawa's approach and assumed that Kurita, like the other survivors of the battle in Surigao Strait, was withdrawing and it was safe to go

after the carriers, which he did, leaving San Bernardino Strait unguarded. Kurita had not fled, however.

Emerging from San Bernardino Strait on the morning of October 25, the Japanese warships attacked six escort carriers, screened by three destroyers and four destroyer escorts, under Rear Adm. Clifton A. F. Sprague. Planes from Sprague's escort carriers and others nearby stung the Japanese, landing ashore to replenish bombs and ammunition, and the warships protecting the carriers laid down a smoke screen and attacked with torpedoes, losing two destroyers and a destroyer escort. After mauling one escort carrier and sinking another, Kurita unaccountably broke off the action.

That same morning, Halsey's aircraft attacked Ozawa, whose 116 planes could offer only token resistance. The airmen sank *Zuikaku* and three other carriers. Meanwhile, urgent calls for help caused Halsey to change course for Leyte instead of pursuing the surviving Japanese ships.

The kamikazes had already attacked the Leyte beachhead, sinking a landing craft and a tug on October 21. Four days later, a kamikaze dived through the flight deck of the escort carrier *St. Lo*, touching off explosions that sank the ship in half an hour. As the liberation of the Philippines proceeded, the suicide planes remained a threat. In December 1944, a kamikaze crashed into the bridge of the cruiser *Nashville*, en route to Mindoro, killing three officers and wounding the commander of the assault troops. At the Mindoro beachhead, suicide pilots hit two LSTs, killing 107 of the 750 soldiers on board.

Air power provided cover against the kamikazes, bombed the factories in Japan that manufactured planes for them, and supported operations ashore. On Luzon, invaded in January 1945, C-47s dropped paratroops at Corregidor and Taygaytay Ridge. During the advance toward Manila, Marine SBDs patrolled an open flank of the 1st Cavalry Division and eliminated strongholds in its path. The conquest of Luzon continued throughout the spring, as the bombing of Japan from the Marianas intensified.

Iwo Jima

Meanwhile, the Japanese island of Iwo Jima troubled both Hansell and LeMay. It served the Japanese as an early warning radar site and a staging area for air raids on the Marianas, such as the attack on December 7, 1944, that destroyed three B-29s and damaged twenty-three. In American hands, Iwo Jima would provide airfields for escorting fighters and for B-29s with battle damage or engine trouble.

A Vought F4U Corsair unleashes a barrage of rockets against stubborn Japanese defenders holding out on Okinawa.

Marines stormed the island on February 19, 1945, captured Mount Suribachi and raised the flag there, then fought yard-by-yard to conquer the island. Ironically, a Japanese attack launched after Iwo Jima was officially secure posed the greatest danger to the Army Air Forces support troops operating one of the airfields. The enemy penetrated the security screen to kill and wound dozens of soldiers and airmen in the tents where they were sleeping.

Although sporadic fighting continued into April, a captured airfield began operating on March 6. By the end of the war, some 2,000 B-29s, each with an eleven-man crew, had landed there, prompting Adm. King to suggest that Iwo Jima saved more lives than the 6,000 lost in capturing it. Of course, not every B-29 landing there would otherwise have crashed at sea.

Fire Bombs and Atomic Weapons

In stepping up the severity of his attacks, LeMay decided in March to avoid the jet stream, the scattering of incendiaries that had hampered the earlier high-altitude fire raids, and the strain on engines caused by climbing to

RIGHT, TOP: Col. Paul W. Tibbetts, Jr., waves from the cockpit of the B-29 *Enola Gay* before taking off from Tinian to drop an atomic bomb on Hiroshima. Tibbets would later complain that his name became so firmly linked to atomic destruction that the public's perception damaged his career. RIGHT, BOTTOM: The mushroom cloud that came to symbolize nuclear weapons towers over Nagasaki, where on August 9, 1945, the B-29 *Bock's Car*, flown by Maj. Charles W. Sweeney, dropped a second atomic bomb, killing and wounding as many as 96,000 persons.

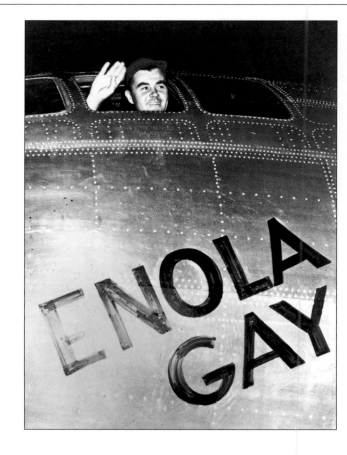

25,000 feet (7,625m) or higher. Convinced that Japanese radar was both ineffective and easily jammed, he chose to attack by night from a low altitude after removing the tail guns from the planes to save weight for additional incendiaries. He no longer bombed industries but the cities themselves, jammed with inflammable wooden homes and lacking modern fire-fighting equipment. On the night of March 9–10, he began systematically to burn Japan's cities, starting with Tokyo, where fires killed more than 83,000 and left a million homeless.

The invasion of Okinawa on April 1 stirred up a hornet's nest of kamikazes and forced LeMay to interrupt his fire-bombing to attack aircraft plants and the airfields the suicide pilots used. To intercept the kamikazes, the Navy established a radar picket line of destroyers, which themselves came under fierce attack, and Army fighter squadrons served alongside marines under the command of a Marine general until the island was declared secure on June 21.

Despite the interruptions, by mid-June the fire-bombing had consumed an area of 250 square miles (648 square km) divided among six cities, though Tokyo suffered the worst. When Japanese antiaircraft fire proved unexpectedly deadly—as on May 25, when a hundred bombers sustained damage and twenty-six failed to return—LeMay reverted to high-altitude daylight attacks. The number of bombers available—five hundred for a mission compared to Hansell's hundred—ensured massive fires. Before handing over the Twentieth Air Force to LeMay, Arnold agreed to use the B-29s for mine-laying to help seal the Navy's blockade of Japan.

The onslaught of the kamikazes and the fierce Japanese resistance on the islands of the Pacific raised concern that an invasion of Japan would result in a bloodbath. The enemy might be further weakened by bombing and blockade, but it was believed only the newly developed atomic bomb seemed likely to shock Japan into surrender without an invasion. President Harry S. Truman, who had assumed office on the death of Roosevelt in April 1945, decided to use the new weapon against Japan.

The 509th Composite Group, under Col. Paul W. Tibbets, Jr., had trained since January to drop the bomb from its B-29s. On August 6, Tibbets, flying *Enola Gay*, an aircraft named after his mother, destroyed the city of Hiroshima. A Japanese government, divided among its warriors and peacemakers, could not unite to consider seriously Truman's demand to surrender.

Japan's indecision reinforced the vision of a kamikaze nation willing to fight to the death, and the United States commander in chief authorized the dropping of a second atomic bomb. Maj. Charles W. Sweeney, flying a borrowed B-29 named *Bock's Car*, took off for Kokura on August 9, found it covered by cloud, and bombed Nagasaki instead.

The two atomic strikes—which killed 100,000 or more by blast, fire, and radiation—forced Emperor Hirohito to defy tradition; instead of acting as spokesman for his cabinet, he told the group that the time for surrender had come. A consensus for surrender gradually emerged, but in the meantime Truman, after having suspending bombing on August 11, concluded

that Japan might continue fighting and authorized further bombing for August 14. The thousand fighters and B-29s that raided Japan were returning to their bases when word came from Washington that Japan had agreed to surrender.

After almost six years and an incalculable expenditure of blood and wealth, the air war had ended. Air power had not brought swift victory, but it did expand the battlefield to include the entire population, homes, shops, and factories. Both civilian morale, sometimes backed by totalitarian discipline, and war industries, including oil production, proved more resilient than expected.

The atomic bomb, however, seemed the decisive weapon that would enable the air arm to fulfill Giulio Douhet's vision of an independent air force armed with battle planes capable of fighting their way to vital targets and destroying them to win a war without the aid of naval and ground forces.

On September 2, 1945, a Japanese delegation headed by Mamoru Shigemitsu (with cane) and Gen. Yoshijiro Umezu arrives on the deck of the battleship *Missouri* to sign the articles of surrender. The war that began with an American defeat at Pearl Harbor ended in victory at Tokyo Bay.

Bibliography

Arakaki, Leatrice R., and John Kuborn. *7 December 1941: The Air Force Story.* Hickam Air Force Base, Hawaii: Pacific Air Forces Office of History, 1991.

Arnold, Henry H. *Global Mission.* New York: Harper, 1949.

Babington-Smith, Constance. *Air Spy: The Story of Photo Intelligence in World War II.* New York: Ballantine, 1957.

Beck, Earl R. *Under the Bombs: The German Home Front, 1942–1945.* Lexington: University of Kentucky, 1986.

Bekker, Cajus. *The Luftwaffe War Diaries.* Garden City, New York: Doubleday, 1968.

Bendiner, Elmer. *The Fall of the Fortresses: A Personal Account of the Most Daring and Deadly American Air Battles of World War II.* New York: G. P. Putnam's Sons, 1980.

Berger, Carl. *B-29: The Superfortress.* New York: Ballantine, 1970.

Boyne, Walter J. *Clash of Wings: World War II in the Air.* New York: Simon and Schuster, 1994.

Byrd, Martha. *Chennault: Giving Wings to the Tiger.* Tuscaloosa: University of Alabama, 1988.

Coffey, Thomas M. *Decision over Schweinfurt: The U. S. 8th Air Force Battle for Daylight Bombing.* New York: David McKay, 1977.

———. *Hap: The Story of the U. S. Air Force and the Man Who Built It, General "Hap" Arnold.* New York: Viking, 1982.

———. *Iron Eagle: The Turbulent Life of General Curtis LeMay.* New York: Crown, 1986.

Copp, Dewitt S. *Forged in Fire: Strategy and Decisions in the Air War over Europe, 1940–1945.* New York: Doubleday, 1982.

Corum, James S. *The Luftwaffe: Creating the Operational Air War, 1918–1940.* Lawrence: University Press of Kansas, 1997.

Craven, Wesley Frank, and James L. Cate, eds. *The Army Air Forces in World War II*, 7 vols. Washington, D.C.: Office of Air Force History, reprinted 1983.

Davis, Benjamin O., Jr. *An Autobiography: Benjamin O. Davis, Jr., American.* Washington, D.C.: Smithsonian Institution, 1992.

Davis, Richard G. *Carl A. Spaatz and the Air War in Europe.* Washington, D.C.: Center for Air Force History, 1993.

Doolittle, James H., with Carrol V. Glines. *I Could Never Be So Lucky Again: An Autobiography by General James H. "Jimmy" Doolittle.* New York: Bantam, 1991.

Dornberger, Walter. *V-2.* New York: Viking, 1954.

Douhet, Giulio. *The Command of the Air*, translated by Dino Ferrari. Washington, D.C.: Office of Air Force History, reprinted 1991.

Dugan, James, and Carrol Stewart. *Ploesti: The Great Air-Ground Battle of 1 August 1943.* New York: Random House, 1962.

Edmonds, Walter D. *They Fought with What They Had.* Washington, D.C.: Office of Air Force History, reprinted 1993.

Ethell, Jeffrey. *Mustang: A Documentary History of the P-51.* London: Davis, 1981.

Falk, Stanley. *Decision at Leyte.* New York: Norton, 1966.

Francillon, Rene. *Japanese Aircraft of the Pacific War.* Annapolis: Naval Institute, 1987.

Fredette, Raymond H. *The Sky on Fire: The First Battle of Britain and the Birth of the Royal Air Force.* Washington, D.C.: Smithsonian Institution, reprinted 1991.

Freeman, Roger, with Alan Crouchman and Vic Maslen. *The Mighty Eighth War Diary.* London: Arms and Armour, revised 1990.

Galland, Adolf. *The First and the Last: The Rise and Fall of the German Fighter Forces, 1938–1945.* New York: Henry Holt, 1954.

Green, William. *Warplanes of the Third Reich.* New York: Galahad, 1990.

———. *Warplanes of the Second World War*, 10 vols. Garden City, New York: Hanover House, 1960–1971.

Hall, R. Cargill, ed. *Lightning over Bougainville: The Yamamoto Mission Reconsidered.* Washington, D.C.: Smithsonian Institution, 1991.

Hallion, Richard P. *Strike from the Sky: The History of Battlefield Air Attack, 1911–1945.* Washington, D.C.: Smithsonian Institution, 1989.

Hardesty, Von. *Red Phoenix: The Rise of Soviet Air Power, 1941–1945.* Washington, D.C.: Smithsonian Institution, 1982.

Harris, Sir Arthur. *Bomber Offensive.* New York: Macmillan, 1947.

Hinton, Harold B. *Air Victory: The Men and the Machines.* New York: Harper, 1948.

Holley, Irving B. *Buying Aircraft: Materiel Procurement for the Army Air Forces.* Washington, D.C.: Office of Chief of Military History, 1964.

Homze, Edward L. *Arming the Luftwaffe: The Reich Air Ministry and the Aircraft Industry, 1919–1939.* Lincoln: University of Nebraska, 1976.

Hough, Richard, and Denis Richards. *The Battle of Britain: The Greatest Air Battle of World War II.* New York and London: New York: Norton, 1989.

Infield, Glenn. *Big Week.* New York: Pinnacle, 1974.

———. *The Poltava Affair: A Russian Warning; An American Tragedy.* New York: Macmillan, 1973.

Inoguchi, Rikihei, Tadashi Nakajima, and Roger Pineau. *The Divine Wind: Japan's Kamikaze Force in World War II.* Annapolis: Naval Institute, 1958.

Jones, R. V. *The Wizard War: British Scientific Intelligence, 1939–1945.* New York: Coward, McCann and Geoghegan, 1978.

Jones, Vincent. *MANHATTAN: The Army and the Atomic Bomb.* Washington, D.C.: Center of Military History, 1985.

Kennett, Lee. *A History of Strategic Bombing.* New York: Charles Scribner's Sons, 1982.

Kenney, George C. *General Kenney Reports: A Personal History of the Pacific War.* Washington, D.C.: Office of Air Force History, reprinted 1987.

Lewin, Ronald. *American Magic: Codes, Ciphers, and the Defeat of Japan.* New York: Farrar, Straus, Giroux, 1982.

———. *Ultra Goes to War: The First Account of World War II's Greatest Secret, Based on Official Documents.* New York: McGraw-Hill, 1978.

Lukas, Richard. *Eagles East: The Army Air Forces and the Soviet Union.* Tallahassee: Florida State University, 1970.

Masatake, Okumiya, Jiro Horikoshi, and Martin Caidin. *Zero.* New York: E. P. Dutton, 1956.

McFarland, Stephen L., and Wesley Phillips Newton. *To Command the Sky: The Battle for Air Superiority over Germany, 1942–1944.* Washington, D.C.: Smithsonian Institution, 1991.

McGovern, James. *Crossbow and Overcast.* New York; Morrow, 1964.

McKee, Alexander. *Dresden, 1945: The Devil's Tinderbox.* New York: E. P. Dutton, 1984.

Middlebrook, Martin. *The Battle of Hamburg: Allied Bomber Forces against a German City in 1943.* New York; Charles Scribner's Sons, 1980.

———. *The Nuremberg Raid, 30–31 March 1944.* New York: William Morrow, 1973.

———. *The Schweinfurt-Regensburg Mission.* New York: Charles Scribner's Sons, 1983.

Mierzejewski, Alfred C. *The Collapse of the German War Economy, 1944–1945: Allied Air Power and the German National Railway.* Chapel Hill: University of North Carolina, 1988.

Muirhead, John. *Those Who Fall.* New York: Random House, 1986.

Murray, Williamson. *Strategy for Defeat: The Luftwaffe, 1933–1945.* Maxwell Air Force Base, Alabama: Air Power Research Institute, 1983.

Orange, Vincent. *Coningham: A Biography of Air Marshal Sir Arthur Coningham, KCB, KBE, DSO, MC, DFC, AFC.* Washington, D.C.: Center for Air Force History, reprinted 1992.

Osur, Alan. *Blacks in the Army Air Forces during World War II.* Washington, D.C.: Office of Air Force History, 1977.

Overy, R. J. *The Air War, 1939–1945.* New York: Stein and Day, 1981.

Park, Edwards. *Nanette.* New York: Norton, 1977.

Parrish, Thomas. *The Ultra Americans: The U. S. Role in Breaking the Nazi Codes.* New York: Stein and Day, 1986.

Parton, James. *"Air Force Spoken Here": General Ira Eaker and the Command of the Air.* Bethesda, Maryland: Adler and Adler, 1986.

Perret, Geoffrey. *Winged Victory: The U. S. Army Air Forces in World War II.* New York: Random House, 1993.

Prange, Gordon W., with Donald M. Goldstein and Katherine V. Dillon. *At Dawn We Slept: The Untold Story of Pearl Harbor.* New York: McGraw-Hill, 1981.

———— . *Miracle at Midway.* New York: McGraw-Hill, 1982.

Price, Alfred. *Instruments of Darkness: The History of Electronic Warfare.* London: MacDonald and Jane's, 1978.

Richards, Denis. *The Fight at Odds, vol. I, Royal Air Force, 1939–1945.* London: Her Majesty's Stationery Office, 1953.

Richards, Denis, and Hilary St.G. Saunders. *The Fight Avails, vol. II, Royal Air Force, 1939–1945.* London: Her Majesty's Stationery Office, 1954.

Saunders, Hilary St.G. *The Fight Is Won, vol. III, Royal Air Force, 1939–1945.* London: Her Majesty's Stationery Office, 1954.

Saward, Dudley. *Bomber Harris: The Story of Sir Arthur Harris, Marshal of the Royal Air Force.* Garden City, New York: Doubleday, 1985

Sherrod, Robert L. *History of United States Marine Corps Aviation in World War II.* San Rafael, California: Presidio Press, reprinted 1984.

Speer, Albert. *Inside the Third Reich*, translated by Richard and Clara Winston. New York: Macmillan, 1970.

Terraine, John. *A Time for Courage: The Royal Air Force in the European War, 1939–1945.* New York: Macmillan, 1985.

Thomas, Gordon, and Max Morgan Witts. *Enola Gay.* New York: Stein and Day, 1977.

Tibbets, Paul W., Jr., with Claire Stebbins and Harry Franken. *The Tibbets Story.* New York: Stein and Day, 1967.

Webster, Sir Charles, and Noble Frankland. *The Strategic Air Offensive against Germany*, 4 vols. London: Her Majesty's Stationery Office, 1961.

Y'Blood, William T. *Red Sun Setting: The Battle of the Philippine Sea.* Annapolis: Naval Institute, 1981.

———— . *The Little Giants: U. S. Escort Carriers against Japan.* Annapolis: Naval Institute, 1987.

Photo Credits

The publishers have made every effort to trace the copyright owners of the illustrations in this book, but the nature of the material has meant that this has not always been possible. Any person or organization we have failed to reach, despite our efforts, is invited to contact the Photo Director.

Baldwin H. Ward/Corbis-Bettmann: pp. 68–69, 103

Corbis-Bettmann: pp. 15 both, 29 top, 72 bottom, 73 both, 75, 76, 106, 108, 115

Michael Green Collection: p. 93 both

National Archives and Records Administration: U.S. Navy Photos: pp. 4–5, 10, 16 bottom, 17, 46–47, 49, 50, 54–55 both, 58 bottom, 59 both, 85, 100–101, 112–113 both, 114, 116–117 all; U.S. Air Force Photos: pp. 2–3, 8–9, 14 both, 16 top, 18–19 all, 20 both, 25 both, 27 bottom, 28 both, 35, 36 bottom, 39 top, 41, 42, 43, 51 top, 56 foreground, 57 foreground, 56–57 background, 60, 61 both, 70–71 both, 77, 78, 81, 82–83 (digital retouching by Daniel J. Rutkowski), 86–87 all, 89 both, 90 both, 91, 94–95 both, 96–97 all, 99 bottom, 104, 107, 109, 118; The New York Times Paris Bureau Collection (USIA): pp. 30-31, 38 top; Office of War Information Photo: p. 52; Enemy Captured Film: p. 72 top; U.S. Army Air Forces Photo: pp. 99 top, 120 top; U.S. Marine Corps: pp. 105 bottom, 119; Argonne National Laboratory Photo: p. 120 bottom; U.S. Army Photos: p. 121

UPI/Corbis-Bettmann: pp. 6–7, 11, 12–13, 21, 22–23, 24 both, 26, 27 top, 29 bottom, 33, 34, 36 top, 37, 38 bottom, 39 bottom, 40, 44, 45, 51 bottom, 53, 58 top, 62–63, 64–65 both, 66–67 both, 79 both, 80, 88, 92, 98, 105 top, 110–111 all

Index